INSIDE OUT

To Diane
Good gardening.

[signature]

INSIDE OUT

The Art and Craft of Home Landscaping

text, photos, and illustrations by

JEFF HUTTON

BREAKAWAY BOOKS
HALCOTTSVILLE, NEW YORK
2007

Published by Breakaway Books

P.O. Box 24 Halcottsville, NY 12438

www.breakawaybooks.com

FIRST EDITION

ACKNOWLEDGMENTS

Always, Diane and the kids, without whom none of this would really matter at all.

I think there are few vocations in which you might encounter people more honorable or more dedicated. This work is rarely easy yet always rewarding. There are many people I've come to know along the way who have contributed to my appreciation of this craft and my love of this art. I'll simply mention a few.

Rob Symonds, my friend and associate for many years. An accomplished mason, carpenter, gardener, and supervisor of men—a designer in his own right—he always makes us look good through his patient dedication to this craft.

James Zimmer, Steve Dwyer, Matt Ravetto, and Lou Bach, Jr. have been great students of this work, investing something of themselves in each project.

There are "plantsmen," those who've dedicated a large part of their life to the understanding of plants. Bill Terrell is one of them, and has taught me much about perennials over the last twenty years. Bill and his family are some of the good people in this business. In truth, there are far too many to mention: Jim and Linda Messier, Jim Kelly, an enthusiastic student and advocate of the plant world. Jim Gorman, who worked with me for many years and whose skill and dedication to this craft are admirable, showing up from time to time on these pages in some of our older creations.

And the hundreds of laborers, gardeners, masons, carpenters, and other designers with whom I've been honored to work over these three decades and from whom I continue to learn.

And special thanks to my editor-publisher, Garth Battista, who helped me make sense of all this.

CONTENTS

To

DONALD C. HUTTON, JR.

In loving memory.

MASTER GARDENER
BUSINESS PARTNER
BROTHER
FRIEND

BEGINNINGS

An introduction

And see that we, outlaws on God's property,
Fling out imagination beyond the skies,
Wishing a tangible good from the unknown.
—Richard Eberhart

For nearly three decades I have witnessed reasonable and intelligent people, perfectly capable of designing and decorating the indoor spaces of their homes, dismayed as they venture into the vast blank slate of the yard. Although capable of all kinds of decisions, including wise design choices for the interior of their houses, many homeowners struggle with similar considerations regarding the yard. In my career as a landscape designer I have met with a great variety of people from all walks of life while designing thousands of residential properties. My work has been to help people confront the issues and challenges presented by the "last frontier" of the yard and help them to discover some joy in the process. It has been, for the most part, a labor of love.

This book is meant for all homeowners who are filled with apprehension as they pass through the slider or the atrium door or emerge from the garage into the open spaces to consider the development of their properties, either new or old. It's meant to instill the same enthusiasm and level of comfort with which you developed the inside spaces of your home. By sharing my experience and discussing some basic design concepts—hopefully revealing some of the mysteries of landscape design—this book will enable you to move outside and apply many of the same basic principles with which you were comfortable inside the living room or the den. Essentially this book will take all that creative courage and excitement and turn it "inside out."

The choices and challenges are even greater once we leave the confines of the house, leave the paint and wallpaper behind to consider the empty spaces of the yard. By trying to eliminate some of the apprehensions and provide simple advice on a variety of projects and concerns, this book intends to liberate you to consider the dramatic new landscape or a renovation of the old and tired. Without encumbering you with a lot of reference material, all of which is available at the library or across the internet, I'll sit down with you as I have for three decades in my role as a designer—in the perfectly considered kitchen, or in the beautifully designed and appointed living room—and figure out why we can't do the same thing outside.

Ultimately, of course, we can. Somewhere inside everyone is a vision. The role of *Inside Out* is to liberate this vision and find practical ways to realize it. To put, in a sense, our own signature on this particular piece of the world we call our own: to "fling out imagination beyond the skies."

9

THE EYES HAVE IT

In Defense of Design

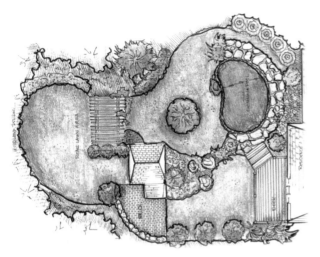

All art is but imitation of nature.
—*Lucius Annaeus Seneca*

I have quite often been humbled, in my years in this business, by the knowledge of the nurseryman, the horticulturist, and even the avid hobby gardeners whom I encounter.

Myself, I've never grown a successful crop of rhubarb or a prize lily or pruned an ancient apple orchard with the care and knowledge that can only come from a lifetime of passionate experience. I know and have worked with masons whose craft is impeccable, arborists who can look up the trunk of a tree and read its life story, expert carpenters who own a lifetime of skills that will never be mine. As a designer, these are all elements that I consider in my work, and to a varying degree I've tried my hand at each one. But being an expert at one or two of the many aspects of gardening and construction does not necessarily add up to a successful landscape. Landscape is the finished product of all these efforts—the "sum of all fears," if you will.

Brief history

Ancient courtyards and terraced gardens, fields of grain or pasture, sculpted vineyards and orchards, the beautifully manicured gardens of royalty and the cottage gardens of the European population—growing flowers, herbs, and vegetables for function as well as pleasant distraction—all of these are ingredients of the American landscape. The influence of the English garden and the formal gardens of the Fench have been part of our evolving American perception and style of landscape. From purely functional to the staid and understated landscapes of the swelling suburbs of post-World War II America, the landscape has changed as much as our culture has changed.

The gardens at Versailles.

The merging of landscapes with the surroundings as well as the structure is an evolving theme. Gertrude Jekyll, the wonderful celebrant of English cottage or country gardens, and Frederick Law Olmsted, who designed Central Park in New York as a veritable oasis in the midst of one of the world's great urban centers in the late 1800s—virtually laying the groundwork for landscape architecture as a serious discipline—both have tremendous influence on the art to this day. Frank Lloyd Wright, merging the surrounding landscape with the structure of the house, was a great proponent of what I call "inside out"—effectively blurring the border between architecture and landscape architecture, or interior and exterior design.

Falling Water by Frank Lloyd Wright

The influence of Lady Bird Johnson and her call for wildflowers everywhere in the late sixties, the infatuation with ornamental grasses in the nineties, a bent toward whimsy in today's garden—all of these show that landscaping follows cultural trends. And since we are a young culture, our landscape and perception of landscape are in an infant stage. The discussion of limited resources, water, or fossil fuel used in the production of many fertilizers influence the evolving landscape. The latest and future battle cry may be the trend toward xerigraphic landscaping, or landscaping that needs very little water.

Because landscape design is, I contend, an art form as much as anything else, it has its own history couched in all of the creative efforts of man: to interpret, or impose something of ourselves on the world.

And in that case, wonderfully—there should be few rules we need to follow.

Landscaping Is More Than Gardening

Gardening is one of the many elements of the landscape. I have known expert nurserymen with unbelievable plant knowledge to come up with questionable landscapes because their knowledge is of specific plants and not their association with one another and the other elements of the landscape. Avid and serious gardeners often select beautiful specimen plants and simply find a place for them. These projects often end up as "look at me" landscapes with little cohesion or harmony, a collection rather than a composition. Quite often the excitement at the color or character of a flower determines its use in the garden rather than any plan. It's as if you go down to the local furniture store and buy all the pieces you like without consideration of any of it going together. Or picking your favorite colors or wallpaper for the walls without thinking of any cohesive overall effect.

I have often thought that given the blank slate of the landscape, a novice homeowner might be better off consulting with the niece or nephew or cousin who just graduated from art school, or a friend with a good eye, than the avid gardner or even botanist. This will come later. A true professional will understand the limitations. Maybe your Aunt Trudy has an attic full of paintings or other art she's been spending a lifetime creating. Give her a call. She might have the eye. In painting the artist calls this preliminary work the *abbozzo,* the first outline or underpainting of the canvas. Your yard is the canvas. *Design is about composition,* no matter what the application.

Beginning the process

If you enjoy putting pencil to paper; if you find yourself doodling imaginatively while talking on the phone; if the margins of your notebook are, or were, filled with bizarre sketches and interlocking shapes—then you are probably very well suited to this phase of the process. It's time to "fling out imagination."

If it's difficult for you, then simply consider the way you may have laid out your living room or den. Look around the house at bold shapes and colors: furniture, rugs, works of art, or knickknacks. You may discover you really do have some sense of design that's yet untapped.

It's best to start with shapes. If you have no experience with this sort of thing, then you might want to take a blank sheet of paper and draw some geometric shapes of varying sizes and type—circles and squares interlocking, for instance. (Does it sound like the margins of your notebook? I thought it might.) This should help you imagine and visualize dynamic space and line. Experiment with different values of pencil line, thick and thin, heavy and light. Experiment with some shading.

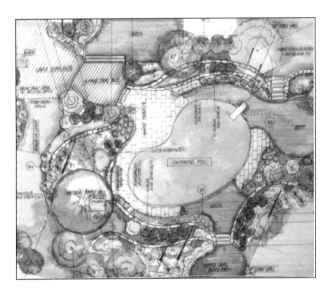

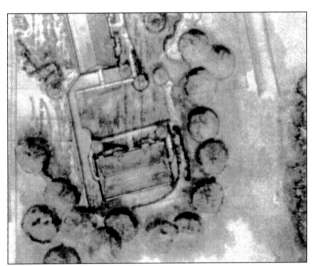

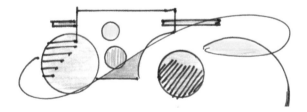

Loosen up with some experimental drawing: "the ab-bozzo." Landscape design is about the relationship of shapes and their successful integration.

If the rest of the family doesn't think you're going off the deep end (and this might be particularly perilous if you have teenagers in the house), do a few of these quick sketches. If you're enjoying it, add some color. This exercise will help you to start thinking in space and line and shape, much like a designer.

Site analysis

The next step is to translate all this creative energy to something practical. It's time for some site analysis. Just as you looked at the empty or unsatisfying spaces of your home when you purchased furniture or painted, it's time now to walk outside and do the same. If you've measured for curtains and figured square footage for paint and wallpaper, you're already an experienced space analyst. Take a cup of coffee or a glass of lemonade and go outside. Walk you property, no matter how large or small. Look out away from the house and back at the structure from the perimeter of the yard. What do you see? Put the lemonade down and start making a few notes, preferably in the same notebook in which you've made all those crazy sketches. This is a wonderful part of the process: beginning to translate practical considerations to creative ideas. It's where you begin to see your yard as a canvas and yourself as the artist.

Make some notes regarding your desires for the yard. What are some of your practical considerations? What are your wildest dreams? Here are some sample notes:

Entertaining. Space for the kids to play. The view from the dining room. Gardens to spend time cultivating. Gardens that need very little time commitment. Cut flowers. Shade or ornamental trees. Privacy screening. Walkways. Patios. Deck. Waterfall. Swimming pool. Volleyball.

You'll need to measure the footprint of the house. This is fairly easily done with a tape measure and perhaps a second set of hands. It's a good time to get together with whomever you share the house with so you know you're thinking along the same lines (quite literally in this case). Notice if the house is symmetrical. Is there a dominant architectural element? Is there an architectural element that needs to be softened or pronounced?

After you've set out a simple line drawing of the house's footprint, it's time to measure the surrounding yard. Measure from the corner or the foundation walls straight out to your property lines or the margins of the space you want to landscape. If you're dealing with a lot of acres, divide the yard into smaller spaces for now. All the pieces can be put together later. Indicate any permanent elements in the space between. If you aren't concerned with very exact measurements, you can simply pace off the yard. The average adult's stride is about three feet. If you want to be sure, measure your own pace by laying out and locking open a retractable tape measure on the ground and walking your natural stride alongside it. Now you've become a tool of your own design method. By counting the number of strides and multiplying by the length of your stride you can measure, fairly accurately, your yard space—certainly accurately enough for this initial design phase.

As far as the existing elements go—trees, boulders and so on—these can be located by measuring via triangulation. With the feature you're trying to locate as one of the three fixed points, find two other fixed points to measure off. This could be the corner of the house and the edge of a door. For accuracy, you can measure a few triangles and be able to locate objects and their relative location.

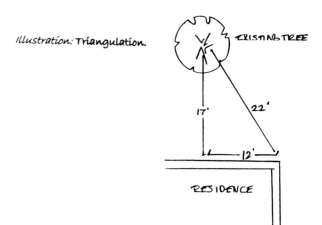

Illustration: Triangulation.

While you're doing all of this walking around, take notice of the sun and the shade. Although the time of the year will determine and alter some of this, you'll begin to understand the exposures. Note the orientation of the house. Which way is north? This is important to planning gardens and in the use and location of decks, patios, and more.

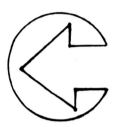

Elevations: One challenge of measuring and analyzing the home landscape is dealing with changes of elevation. If you have a sloping yard, your considerations will be a bit more complicated, although many of the world's most beautiful landscapes are established on multiple levels that can be easily viewed from a variety of vistas.

If the elevation changes aren't severe, you may simply follow the grades with sloping gardens or lawns. If the grade changes are extreme, you may need to build retaining walls to create level terraces. (See "Ups and Downs.") At any rate, at this stage you simply need to indicate the grade change. A professional might use a laser leveling transit. You might want to purchase a simple line level. Set on a string suspended and pinned at ground level and tied to a stake at the lower grade, simply pull the string tight and tie it off when the bubble settles at center and indicates the string is level. By measuring with a tape measure the distance from the string to the ground, you'll know the amount of the grade change. By measuring the distance between the ends of the string line, you can begin to imagine your grade for purposes of design. If you intend to create a level terrace, you may need to construct a retaining wall. With this measurement you'll know how high it will need to be. This height will certainly impact your selection of construction material for the wall. Remember, your wall will need to be slightly lower than the upper terrace grade to allow for positive drainage. You never want to trap water.

Layout: Existing Conditions

Now your paper and notebook are filled with measurement and strange sketches and copious detail notes. When I finish measuring a property my notes are nearly indecipherable to anyone but myself. So no

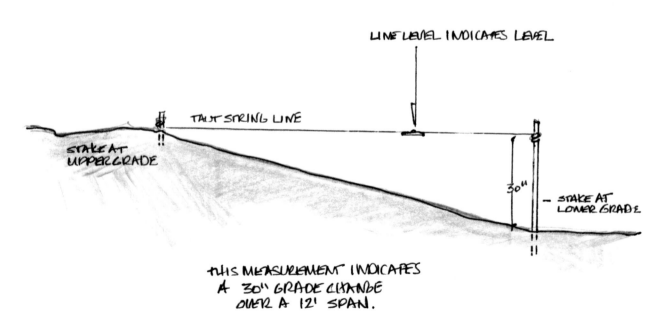

LINE LEVEL INDICATES LEVEL

TAUT STRING LINE

STAKE AT UPPER GRADE

30"

STAKE AT LOWER GRADE

THIS MEASUREMENT INDICATES A 30" GRADE CHANGE OVER A 12' SPAN.

matter how far behind I am in designing, I usually stop to translate the existing conditions of a site fairly quickly to a clean sheet of paper and list all my notes and specifications while they're fresh in my mind.

If you're going to lay things out for yourself—and there are many successful landscape gardeners who skip this stage, I suppose—it's time to have some fun. If you're going to get some help from a friend or artistic or creative relative (if not a professional) it's time to make the call. Whichever is the case, clear a space on the desk or the kitchen table. Get a big roll of drafting paper or large sheets of graph paper. Translate your measurements to a scale drawing of the structure and the yard. If you get quarter- or eighth-inch graph paper or drafting paper, the grid is laid out for you; as you draw your lines with a pencil, every box will indicate an increment of measurement. (Three boxes, for instance, would equal your stride.) When you've translated all of this to paper, creating a scaled-down graphic drawing of your home and property, it might be time to step away from the table. Take some time between the phases of this process. The one you've just finished is fairly mechanical. The next one should be the most creative. It takes a different mind-set, and another walk around the yard or a second lemonade might be just the thing to separate the two.

Landscaping: The Art

It's time to take the shapes and lines and colors you've been sketching and apply them to the paper in front of you. This is the most fun for many—the *purest art* in the process. It's really creative at this point. Don't worry about many practical considerations; they're for the next phase. For now fill the spaces on your paper with line and form, translating the bold strokes of your imagination to the space you've sketched on the paper in front of you. Go back and take a look at those old doodles of yours. Experiment with some new dynamic shapes. Break the open spaces into thirds. Imagine the form of the

house as an integral shape to the whole picture, not merely as a structure. It may be the dominant form of the space, or it may not. Some of these things are now in your hands. Have some fun. Use bold lines and colors. Look at some of your favorite paintings or artwork. Listen to music. You should be "flinging imagination."

Relate your new forms to the existing forms around you. We'll call this (with apologies to Einstein) the Landscaper Theory of Relativity.

Remember. *The eyes have it.*

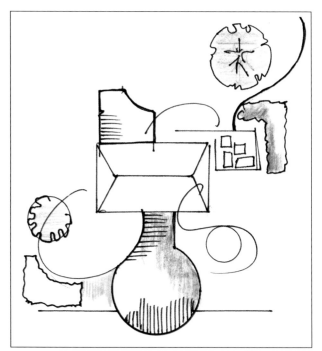

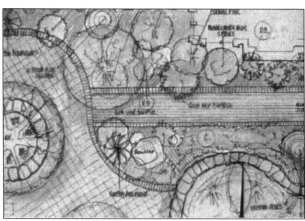

Imagine shape and color: I came across Sol LeWitt's work on the roof of the Metropolitan Museum of Art in New York. Notice the focus on form and color. From a distance anyway, Manhattan seems to be all about form: and relative form at that.

Basic drafting tools: T square, triangle, templates, architectural scale

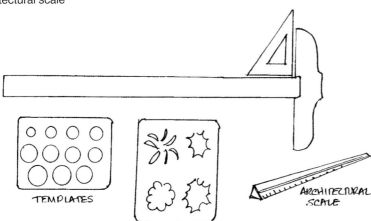

TEMPLATES

ARCHITECTURAL SCALE

Now back to the craft

When you have a visually pleasing composition and you've made some ridiculously inadequate explanation to the rest of the family as to exactly what you're doing, you can get back to the practical. Here is where the volume of information available to you through books and the internet become an important tool to you. As you imagine shapes and sizes— as you begin to fill the empty spaces—you've begun to design your landscape. Now it's time to begin to fill in the details. Don't compromise too much. Cling to your creativity. Perhaps you'll make that circle a patio, even if it's intersected by a square (intruding lawn or garden). Is one of those bold arcs you drew an outline for a walkway, a garden path, or the edge of a garden? Is that oval a pool or a pond? It's time to get practical, and compromise is usually an aspect of this phase. But translating the shapes and lines of your imagination to practical landscape elements is the true art of this wonderful endeavor.

There are hundreds of thousands of plants and trees, paving materials, wall stones, lawn space alternatives, and accents to incorporate in to the residential landscape. It's an industry filled with long-standing tradition and exciting innovation. But only if you've been creative in this initial process might the blanks be effectively and satisfyingly filled in.

17

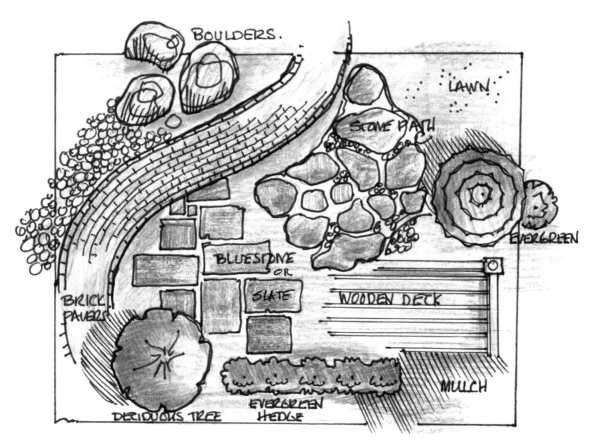

Graphic style: As with any creative endeavor, an individual style develops. There are fairly universal symbols, but they can be translated by the designer in various ways. Done effectively, the design can evoke the atmosphere you're trying to suggest.

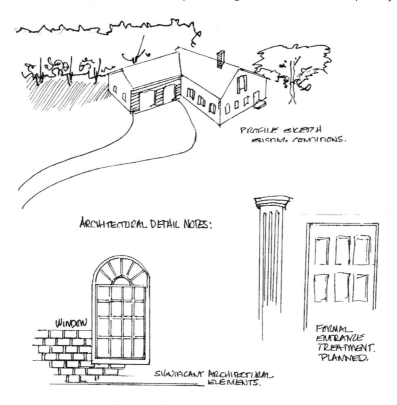

Profiles and line sketches: existing conditions on site. By all means, sweat the details!

Graphics and basic symbols

The previous page offers a few basic images used to represent elements of the landscape. Even if you don't have much drawing ability, these symbols are easy to create and use. I've known people to actually cut out symbols and shapes and manipulate them around the plan like a ouija board. Because of the dynamics, this might be the best way for the novice to experiment in this phase. Cut out basic shapes of trees and shrubs, patios and decks, pools et cetera. Shuffle them around until they work visually. Maybe you'll even receive some divine creative inspiration—or at least hear the voice of a deceased relative. Perhaps Aunt Trudy after all.

If you do have some artistic ability, try some line sketches and three-dimensional profiles. They don't need to be anything but representative of the kind of shape or even plant you're imagining. Remember our version of the Theory of Relativity.

Are we having fun yet? There is an enormous amount to learn and fortunately, an equally enormous amount of knowledge at your fingerprints. Every professional and student of gardening or landscaping has something to offer the homeowner or the novice. But it is more an art than a science. And we're not designing rockets or intricate communication systems. We're simply trying to improve the environment in which we live. This should be both a truly creative and a humbling human experience, with nature almost always the best mentor.

Computers assume an increasing role in this process, but without a fundamental understanding of the creative process, a computer will be a graphic tool. Take all of the information available to you, the priceless knowledge of experienced nurserymen, the gardener, the mason—and put all the knowledge together as you might inside your home. Or find someone to help you put it all together, perhaps Aunt Trudy who has a great eye. Don't hesitate to call her. It's about shapes and form, balance and harmony, color, texture and perspective. It's about all of these elements. It's not about a particular plant or its pathology. It's not about the latest trend in paving material. Landscape design is the association of elements in the environment. It's about the living landscape. Find a designer with a proven track record. Or, better still, become one yourself. Express yourself. Develop your eye. These pages are meant to assist you in that pursuit. Landscaping is an art. Amen.

Perspective profile.

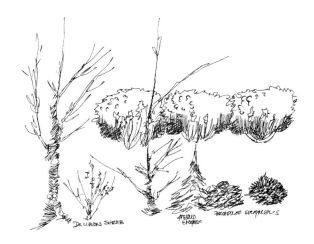

Three dimensional plant profiles: think texture, size and shape.

LANDSCAPE BY DESIGN

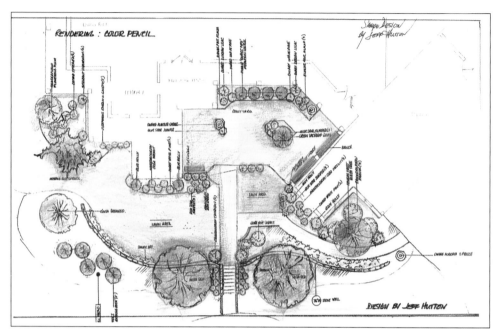

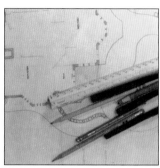

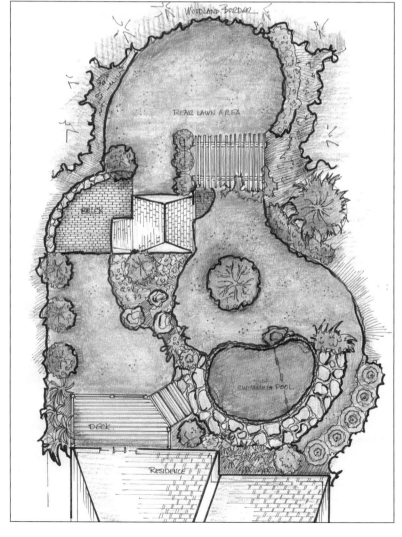

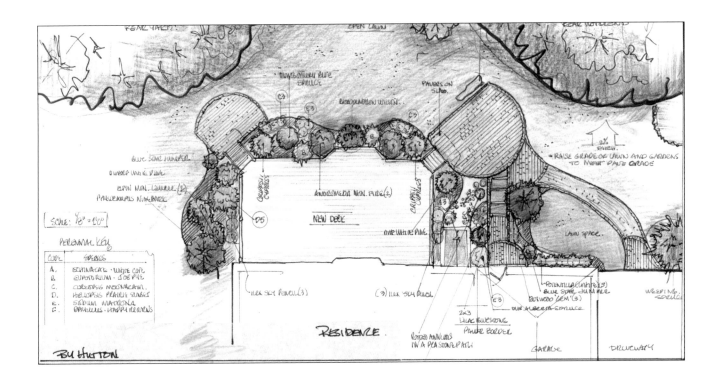

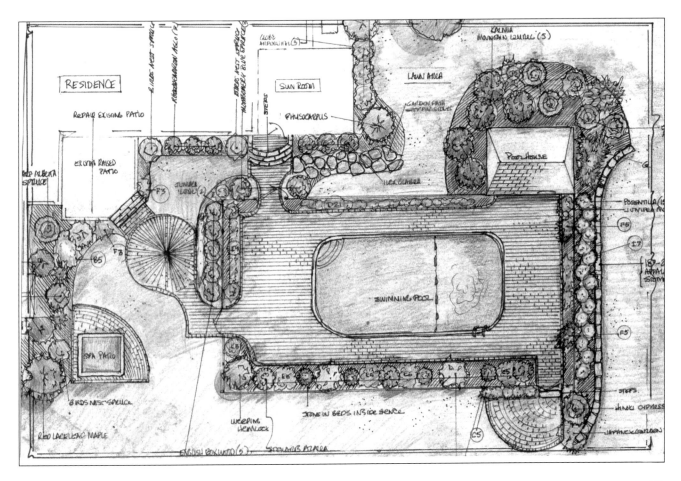

See every component of the conception and installation as
an integral part of the canvas of the imagined landscape.

DRESSED FOR SUCCESS

Foundation beds in the age of
houses without foundations.

*On that bleak hill-top the earth was hard with black
frost, and the air made me shiver through every limb.
Being unable to remove the chain, I jumped over, and
running up the flagged causeway bordered with strug-
gling gooseberry bushes, knocked vainly for admittance,
till my knuckles tingled and the dogs howled."*
—*Emily Brontë,* Wuthering Heights

Old habits are hard to break. In fact, old habits
are often embellished by time and convenience. It has
taken, and will probably take another generation or
two, a great deal of time and energy to break the spell
regarding planting around the house. There is this
image in the minds of many homeowners—a house
surrounded with evergreens. I can draw it in the air.

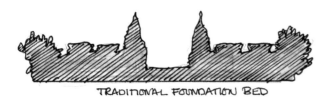

TRADITIONAL FOUNDATION BED

It is the landscape of our parents and our grand-
parents: the heavy massing of yews (*Taxus densiformis*)
and the placement of rhododendron, which you'll
spend a month of Sundays pruning and trying to keep
at bay. And after all the work in establishing and
maintaining these plants, you finally go inside and
look out of the window, and you can't see a damn
thing. Crammed close to the concrete and the siding,
this kind of planting is invisible from inside. Or, if it
is visible, it's overgrown and blocks your view outside.

Most houses constructed in the decades after
World War II were built on raised foundations (no
basements) and this seems to be where our most recent tradition was born. It seemed necessary to line
up plants to hide the concrete. The tradition simply
continued even as foundations shrank in size.

The obscured view The invisible landscape

Well, it's time to shake the shackles of tradition.
Try this. With you or your wife or a friend standing
inside the house, place the first plant—a substantial
one—where it can be seen and admired from inside.
Then work from there.

Remember scale

The size of the front yard, particularly the distance
from the road, is a crucial factor. If you have a small
front yard, you'll need to keep the scale of the plants

smaller. However, the introduction of a forefront garden might actually create the illusion of depth. Most certainly, establishing layers can make the visual context of the structure more complex and compelling.

This might even be more important if the house is architecturally simple or uninteresting. You can manipulate the context and create an exciting environment which makes the clean and simple lines of the home's architecture seem graceful and bold, to stretch the metaphor just a bit—a visual resting place.

You may want to frame the view with plantings.

In the case of the larger front yard—a home set back across a broad expanse of open space or lawn—there are other considerations. You might want to frame the home with plantings. You might want to divide the space (think in thirds, as do most artists) and create an effective forefront and middle ground.

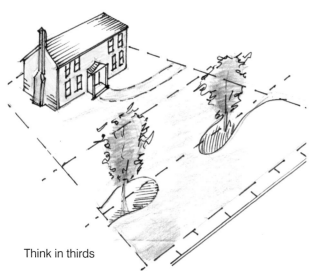

Think in thirds

Perhaps the bold statement of the solitary house is what you want. Think of the southern plantation or the rural New England farmhouse viewed from a distance: The look can be quite striking. That clean plane of lawn may be just the right statement of elegance to create a simple frame and introduction to compelling architecture. However, if the house is small and unassuming, the broad lawn may be accentuating the isolation of the structure. It may make the home appear smaller than it is. This is where the introduction of plantings or other elements such as hardscape can be essential.

In general—and certainly increasingly in practical terms as large lawn spaces become an exhausting drain on natural resources—reducing the front lawn space is probably desirable. The open feel can be achieved in other ways, which will be discussed in subsequent chapters.

The placement of a tree or trees, scaling down the open space into segments of smaller spaces, might be all that's needed. This can be an anchor to a surrounding garden bed. Sometimes an intermediate garden full of small or low plantings can be just right to interrupt sight lines, slowing the eye down across the space toward the house. The advantageous placement of something in the forefront—or bracketing the structure—might visually enlarge the form of the house. Remember, our perception is relative.

We can manipulate the entrance by dragging the walkway into a simple curve, slicing through the broad plane of lawn to create smaller spaces at its edges. These spaces can be left as geometric planes of lawn, or filled with plants and flowers. The chapter on entrance walkways ("The Approach") will elaborate on this, but in the meantime—stand at the curb or sidewalk. Begin to imagine the house in the framework of the landscape. Remember, this process is about the association of elements, and if the house is a finished entity, all the potential rests with the surrounding landscape.

You never get a second chance
to make a first impression.

Before

After

Curb appeal

The apparent siren song of the real estate industry these last few years, *curb appeal* refers to an observer's first impression of the home. It's what really sells the house, or on the other hand, may keep potential buyers from exploring the real estate further. So it makes sense to keep the view from the front, the "public landscape," appealing and compelling.

Identify some simple lines from inside the home. Using stakes or spray paint, locate potential beds so you can enjoy some of your gardens and landscape from inside.

Layering: creating depth in the foundation bed

Not to be confused with a specific way to propagate plants, layering is one of the easiest and most effective ways to create depth, and therefore visual interest

We routinely layer forms inside the home.

Layering the garden: Think geometrically. Size, form, color, and texture should be considered.

in the foundation bed. Simply put, plants are established in ascending size from front to back. Varying foliage and form creates even more interest.

The eye is drawn in across the layers of plants. To begin with, think of the space in geometric terms and research to fill the emptiness with form and interest. Consider form, size, or "habit" of the plants that you'll use to fill the space. Foliage color and texture are important to consider as well as you can create tremendous interest with variation.

Architectural form and balance

Artistic balance doesn't mean perfect symmetry—although it might. Artistic balance is the comfortable division and separation of shape and form and size. For instance, one large evergreen might balance three small flowering shrubs. A single plant can work toward balancing an elaborate perennial garden full of a hundred plants. Balance is a visual comfort, not a static division toward equal parts.

Although not equal, the position of the images creates balance. The image of the woman is balanced by the image of the bridge that the American impressionist Theodore Robinson painted in the background. The "weight" of the images is comparable, if not equal. Balance is not necessarily symmetry.

Foundation beds can be drawn out into the yard to help connect space rather than drawing a line of demarcation between the structure and the lawn. Pulling a graceful line from the corner and creating a peninsula garden helps connect and unify the spaces. Another advantage to drawing the garden away from the structure is that the garden can be viewed from inside the house rather than cowering beneath the windowsills and emerging only in overgrown foliage that needs to be snipped off.

The front yard becomes a living space—an active part of the landscape.

27

Integration

This will be a major theme. I've come to the conclusion that integration is the key. *It's the intersection of the spaces and elements we see that are the most important.* They can be a visual relief or visually annoying. They include the architecture of the house, the flat horizontal plane of the yard (at least where it intersects the base of the house or foundation), the relationship with the surrounding landscape: wide open or dense and wooded? Urban or rural?

However you approach the landscape of the front yard, do it with careful consideration. *Why are you doing it if it's not to enhance the appearance of the structure and its association with the grounds?* I've noticed over the years an obsession with planting shrubs in front of new houses, as if it were somehow mandatory: a rite of passage for new homeowners. There's that hurried line of evergreens or a bunch of shrubs in full flower at the garden center in spring. As if your mother was going to show up and say, "Oh, yes. You've arrived. You've a big pink rhododendron under your bay window just as your father and I always had."

And then it occurs to you, "Isn't that the one you had to have removed with a dozer and they tore up the whole lawn that summer and hit the water line—"

"Anyway," she'll most likely interrupt, "It looks lovely."

And for now, she's absolutely right. It looks lovely. But it won't for long. No matter how small and delicate they appear when you first bring them home, there are many species of rhododendrons that mature at twenty feet in height, with equal breadth. They can sort of mimic the difference between the sweet infant you bring home from the hospital and the six-foot-four-inch college student who wants the car keys.

Fortunately, a great deal of effort in the green industry has gone into developing or cultivating dwarf or compact plants. There are many plants from which you can choose that are appropriate planted beneath your windows or framing your entrance. I hope, in other chapters, you'll be inspired to think out of the box when planning your formal or public landscape: the front yard.

Remember: "You never get a second chance to make a first impression."

THE CRAFT

ESTABLISHING FOUNDATION BEDS

Preparation: Take your time laying out the beds.

Check your grades to make sure you have positive drainage from the foundation. Check your exposure (the sunlight your garden will get). This might influence size and shape. Once you're happy with both of these factors, you can start edging the garden.

Take a straight or square-edged shovel and kick a deep line where you've painted out your shape. If there is established lawn in this area, the grass will most likely have to be removed. If the grass is thin and weak, you might be able to till the entire area, simply turning the weak grass into the topsoil, where it will eventually decay.

Make a judgment regarding the quality of the soil. If it clings together into a wad when you squeeze it in your hand, it has decent clay content. If it falls through your fingers, its content might be sand or gravel. All soil is a composition of minerals, organic material, and living organisms. It is the degree of each that varies greatly.

You can have soil tested in most areas of the country through county or state programs. The acidity and nutrient content of soil vary greatly. If yours is poor, you may want to order soil by the yard (twenty-seven cubic feet per cubic yard) and have it delivered to the site.

Using this topsoil, begin to form your beds. I think any bed should be raised a few inches if possible. This allows good soil around the roots but ensures that water will shed rather than stand. The rear of the bed—against the foundation if there is one—should be higher than the front so the water sheds away. A raised bed with a cleanly cut edge creates a distinctive form in the landscape. This might be nearly as important as the plants you choose to incorporate in the new beds.

Soil amendments: If you have a compost pile, this is the time to mix it into the bed. If you've had your soil tested and it's acid, you may want to add some limestone, although many ornamental shrubs prefer slightly acidic soil. Shrubs and trees, unlike lawn grasses, are not very fussy about soil. Drainage and an ability to retain moisture are probably more important in the shrub bed. If your soil is sandy and/or rocky, you should add some peat moss or peat humus as you improve the soil. If the soil is heavy with clay, you might want to turn a sandy soil into the mix.

Once you've got your bed prepared, rake the surface smooth and you'll be ready to place your plants. Hopefully you have some kind of design and can place the plants accordingly. It's time to stand back and admire your selection. Educate yourself as to the mature sizes of the plants and try to imagine them fifteen or twenty years down the road. If you've done some homework, you're ready to plant.

Remember, you'll displace a lot of soil as you add the new root systems to the bed. This displaced soil should be broadcast along the surface of the bed or removed completely. The topsoil is usually much better than the lower-layer subsoil. The deeper you get, the more likely you are to want to discard what you find.

Planting: Plant same species at a single time to assure that your placement will work out. And plant shrubs or trees that are balancing each other in tandem. Remember, if you hit that buried ledge in one spot, it might mean moving everything, or at least the associated plants. Container shrubs are often quite root-bound. As you slide the rootball out of the container or basket, you may need to break it up a little to get the feeder roots unwound and exposed. If you're not sure, check with a local nurseryman. Once you've planted everything, move through the garden and tamp the soil down around the new root systems to remove air pockets. Do a final rake with a steel toothed "rock rake" and the new bed will be finished. It's time to soak the roots of the new shrubs.

If you choose to mulch, shredded bark will help keep the soil cool and moist through arid weather, and warmer during frigid weather. You may have some weeding in this initial period—all healthy topsoil (or loam) has some weed content that you've just stirred up. But control the initial wave and you should have control of the garden. Mulch helps this tremendously.

Presentation is everything.

COLOR VALUES
How to "invest" color in your landscape

"In the last years of [Monet's] life, he came to see the garden as more than a simple motif; he came to see it as a work of art in itself, a composition of subtle combinations of colors that he himself had imagined. Life and art became one."

—A Day in the Country: Impressionism and
the French Landscape
(The Los Angeles Country Museum of Art)

Color is at the heart of much artistic expression, and there has rarely been a rule regarding the use of color that has gone unbroken. Color can be exciting, annoying, distracting, or quieting depending on its use. Many volumes have been written on the nature and use of color both inside the home and out, so I'll keep this brief.

With apologies to New York Met fans, I've never been able to handle the orange seats of Shea Stadium. They somehow offend. Orange seems to be the least loved color in the landscape. But like so many other things, color choice is subject to opinion. And within a certain framework most colors can work just fine.

Simple color theory

Discussions of color theory usually begin with this simple palette. *Rainbow:* Colors of the rainbow occur in the following order: red, orange, yellow, green, blue, violet.

These are the colors you might see on a color wheel. Which colors are considered harmonious or conflicting and contradicting is often open to debate, and for our purposes this debate isn't necessary. We simply need to understand which colors look nice in the garden and how their use helps accomplish landscape goals.

Color can be used to draw attention away from space or form as well as toward it. Color can be a focus or a framework.

The cool colors: green, turquoise blue, violet

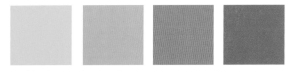

The hot colors: yellow, orange, red, crimson

Hue refers to the particular color, separate and distinct. The primary colors—yellow, blue and red—can be combined to form most other hues.

Value is the relative lightness or darkness of an area of color. In the garden this can be influenced by the amount of sunlight or shade.

Saturation is the purity or brightness of the color. In the landscape this can also be greatly affected by the amount of sunshine that falls across the color. The saturation or intensity of the color can be subdued by associating it with grays, silvers, or blues.

Advancing: The warm colors are considered advancing: as the human eye adjusts to them, they appear to be closer, or in the forefront of other colors. *Receding* colors are cooler colors: blue and green, for instance. These can be used to create the illusion or the reinforcement of depth and distance. Painters do this all the time to create illusion on the flat plane of the canvas.

Complementary colors are opposite colors on the color wheel, like red and green. *Discordant* colors can be the annoying ones, on the other side of the spectrum, but not exact opposites. Think purple and orange.

Balance: Warm and/or advancing colors can outweigh receding or cool colors, so smaller areas of warm colors can balance larger areas of cool colors. Balance is not always symmetry. Think in terms of weight instead of size. A tiny piece of metal can balance a huge empty cardboard box, right? A small splash or red might balance a sea of silver.

Think about how color affects related space. In painting, untreated areas that absorb color are called *absorbent ground.* This is a perfect application of the term as color impacts the surrounding area.

Plants As Color

Basic foliage colors include green, light green, dark green, red, burgundy, purple, gold or yellow, silver or gray, or variegated (multicolored)—and more.

Blue Star Juniper and Rheingold Arborvitae

There's something perfect about this Mountain Laurel flower silhouetted against its own foliage.

All art is an imitation of nature. And nature bursts with spring color. The lime green of early leaf buds opening across the canopy of the varied trees of our woodlands slowly closes the airy windows into the natural landscape, turning the forest floor deep green, with perfect pools of muted hues and the promise of summer shade. Notice the subtle variety. Pale yellow and gold fringe the seedpods and new leaves. The great spruce trees of our woodlands are turning silver, providing a nearly blue edge torn across the spring

Japanese Blood Grass (Imperata)

skyline. It's nature at its best. And most of it is accomplished without the vibrant color of flowers. Except for the thin dogwoods along the woodland edge and a burst of early-blooming mountain laurel, most of this show is produced with a variety of foliage and varied growth habits. Perfect timing. It's a great lesson for the home landscape: subtlety at its best. The true "color value" may be in the use of foliage variety to achieve color in the landscape.

Most of us garden rather impulsively, and many of us do a great deal of our planting in spring. There's nothing at all wrong with this—except that we are too often drawn only to the vivid color of azaleas and the many other spring-blooming shrubs and flowers. The colors of annual flowers are too hard to resist after a long gray winter. We excitedly load our trunk full of reds and purples and everything in between. But I urge you take a moment as you do this to consider the tones of green, yellow, and silver across the shrub yard at most garden centers or nurseries. Try to look away from the bright blooms and appreciate the subtle variation of new growth across the evergreens and flowering shrubs. In almost all cases we live with the foliage much longer than the flower. The foliage has tremendous staying power.

The new growth of andromeda (*pieris japonica*)

The purple foliage of Smoke Bush (*Cotinus*)

A garden of mixed and layered evergreens

The silver-foliage evergreens—many varieties of spruces and junipers—can be used for high visual impact in a foundation bed or as a calming or binding element in a garden robust with bright reds and purples. Mimicking the color of the summer sky, the new growth of some of these evergreens is brilliant and attractive.

Blue Star Juniper (juniperus squamata)

Look at Montgomery blue spruce (Picea pungens 'R.H.Montgomery'). The new growth in spring is a beautiful complement to the deep red of flowering azalea (Rhododendron 'Hino crimson').

Blue Star Juniper (*Juniperus squamata* 'Blue Star') is an example of the many plants that can be used to brighten an evergreen planting or connect a flower garden, separating color masses while soothing the eye. Although the new growth can be breathtaking, the foliage year-round maintains a good silver hue that creates interest through the seasons. Planted at an entrance or an area to which you want attention drawn, these plants can serve you well with their high visual impact. Established in a garden they can serve to bind varied elements and colors; even different themes.

Gold- or yellow-foliage evergreens can be used to brighten partially shaded gardens. Although most evergreens literally pale in the shade (they lose some of their color value), a partially sunny garden will support many of the gold cypresses and other yellow-tinged evergreens. These can be used to draw the eye to the garden or provide a wonderful background to bright reds and oranges—or they'll brighten up a garden filled with whites and pale yellows. Even the foliage color of flowering plants is brought out when offset by gold evergreens.

Gold cypress (*chamaecyparis*)

Rheingold arborvitae (*Thuja* 'Rheingold')

Even when not in bloom, the sharp green blades of perennial foliage such as iris will jump out in front of that soft gold background. And the texture contrast will be equally interesting. Mother Lode Juniper (*Juniperus* 'Mother Lode') can serve as a nice forefront to a garden like this. It stays completely prostrate, grows very slowly (unlike many junipers), and can be used to repeat the gold foliage and create a nice harmony and balance.

Mother Lode Juniper (*Juniperus* 'Mother lode')

Red or burgundy foliage: Perhaps most riveting can be the introduction of red or burgundy foliage into the landscape. Used sparingly because of its impact, the leaves of red maples (*Acer palmatum artropurpureum*) and the many varieties thereof, purple leaf sand cherry (*Prunus* x. *cistena*), and ninebark (*Physocarpus* var.) can be wonderful accents. Combined with silvers—either of these evergreens or the many silver-foliage perennials and ornamental grasses—these gardens can have tremendous interest without depending on a passing bloom. The added bonus is that many of these also bloom. Now, that's a real treat. Sort of like: *Buy one, get one free*.

Using Color

We use color as almost a second nature inside the home. We know, for instance, that bright or bold colors can make a small room feel even smaller. Sometimes it's a desired effect: *Cozy,* we call it. Light or neutral colors can make a room appear larger. There are shades of red that are supposed to inspire appetite. Pastel colors seem to calm the nerves. All of these things can be applied in the landscape through the use of both foliage and flower color, as well as via many of the other elements.

Color is one of the most important elements of any landscape. Nature provides us with a rainbow of varying values from bright red to pale yellow or white, and botanists and nurserymen have cultivated a thousand more variations on all of these. But while we are drawn to this wonderful display of flower color, let's not ignore the foliage. The flowers can be intermittent and brief. The foliage is constant, at least during the growing season. And the color evolves constantly as the growth continues and the intensity of the sunlight alters through the seasons. *Nature is the artist.*

In this sense, as we purchase color for our landscape—evergreens and shrubs with varied-color foliage—we may get more bang for our buck. These considerations may provide the true color "values."

Look to the artists who've spent a lifetime experimenting and understanding color. Colors like red, bright yellow, orange and bright white may seem closer than they are (advancing). These may be called warm or even hot colors.

Pastels or washed colors are visually retreating, they can push the boundary away:

Degas

Landscape

The same colors go together in nature and in the garden as in our clothing or interior design. We might not have an orange couch and purple curtains in the same room . . . or even the same view. The same applies to gardens. However, there are exceptions. At times in the garden strange combinations can look quite beautiful. We also have the benefit and challenge of season and sequence. Certain colors might not appear at the same time as others. Some overlap only slightly. The colors themselves will change drastically as they're saturated with sunlight or drawn with shade. This is why landscape design is as much an art, if not moreso, as it is a science.

You probably do this routinely inside the house. Think about it when you work on the outside.

Dynamic colors or hot colors: (red, orange) can excite, draw attention. Rich red colors are said to excite the appetite and be used in kitchens or dining areas.

Cool colors (blue, pink, silver, pale yellow, white) may be more relaxing, calming.

Yellows and whites can be used to brighten up shady spots or bind other colors. Whites show up on moonlit nights to wonderful effect.

Joan Miró painting   A garden

The art of using color in the garden is as complex as in any art form The plants that provide such beautiful color also provide form, texture, shape, mass, size . . . making landscape design even more challenging than painting with watercolors or shaping clay. And—to further complicate things—they are forever changing.

Color and form come together in the effective landscape.

Landscape

Acrylic on canvas, Jeff Hutton

COLOR VALUES

Forever changing.

CAVEAT EMPTOR

Breaking the Linnaeus Code

"What's in a name?" cries Juliet, "That which we call a rose by any other word would smell as sweet."
—*William Shakespeare*

Buyer Beware: Understanding Plant Nomenclature

You are at the local nursery or garden center. You find a nice plant—an evergreen you're told. (There's something implicitly wonderful about the term *evergreen*—as if anything besides your mortgage will last forever.) A young man helps you carry it and load it into your trunk. Maybe you tip him and go inside to pay for it, carrying the tag.

"*Chamaecyparis filifera obtusifolia,*" the girl behind the counter proudly states as if she is saying the Yankees won or there's a chance of rain on Sunday. You nod weakly, having been reduced with those words to a child-like wonder. When you get home, you lift the plant out and place it in that spot you all thought an evergreen would look wonderful. When your wife comes out she smiles, puts her hands on her hips, and admires the selection.

"It's nice. What is it?"

You fish through the pockets of your jeans until you find that plastic tag. You hesitate.

"Kamacracus filifolia." Stated with elegance and assurance. There is a moment when it works. When her eyes remain fixed on yours like the first time you told her you loved her. And then she breaks a smile. Then she laughs. She laughs so hard that she has to bend over and props her hands on her knees. And there's nothing you can do but join her. Because as much as you know about computers, or international finance, or investment banking, or carpentry, or whatever it might be that you have come to know well and has enabled you to buy this house and property, you know you will never have an inkling of the proper name for this plant.

Well, here's a little help—a cheater's guide, if you will.

The Linnaeus Code

The Latin names assigned to plants are part of an international nomenclature first assigned them or at least organized by the Swedish botanist Carl Linnaeus in the eighteenth century and slowly adopted as the universal language of plants. Even the name *Linnaeus* is a latinized version of his family name, Linné. He wrote 180 books on the natural sciences, with his greatest and most enduring contribution the design of the system of nomenclature for the plant world.

These Latin names when first encountered can be intimidating. But once the system is broken down it's not overwhelming. The name listed first is the genus, and there may be no easy way to remember many of these. But the species names appear after the genus. These are definers, adjectives. And many are fairly easily translatable. Without studying horticulture, recognizing some of these common modifiers can help unveil the mystery that surrounds the plant world—an effort to tell the truth—and turn it into a tool for the new homeowner, the consumer: you, for instance. In L. H. Bailey's book *How Plants Get Their Names*, the author states: "The naming of plants under the system of nomenclature is an effort to tell the truth. Its purpose is not to serve the convenience of those who sell plants or write labels or edit books, it is not commercial. Serving the truth it thereby serves everybody."

And uh, yes. That would include you.

This system replaced an ancient vernacular and is used in place of common names or slang today. Plants have through history been called various things in various locations and cultures. This system, however, is universal. Obviously, this is not the book in which to study the whole system, and I would not be the one to begin to teach it —I'm a lifelong student of it myself. For residential landscaping and gardening, though, it is really helpful to understand some of this—the genus and the species in particular.

Harry Lauder's walking stick (*Corylus avellana* 'Contorta')

Gold Cypress (*chamaecyparis*) and Weigelia in the nursery.

Take a look at the plant pictured here. *Contorta* tells it all doesn't it? Harry Lauder was an old vaudevillian well known for his crooked walking stick. The cultivar name *contorta* is quite descriptive.

Some common names are great, quite colorful and often descriptive. They can even evoke childhood memories: Most grandmas or grandpas had a favorite plant and a clever name for it. However, it's the Latin that clarifies the plants and crosses all language and cultural borders. Obviously the plant your mom might have called Peggy's Sunburst might have a completely different name in Swahili if it also grows on the African continent. But the Latin name would be identical, universal. Whether a common language or a universal confusion, it's just language. And language is power, right?

You don't really need to know too much of this to successfully garden. But what you do know will help you both in understanding plants and in the selection thereof. The following is meant to be an introduction and clarification. Although this is just a tip of the iceberg, my hope is that it might remove some of the mystery if we look at a few Latin modifiers. These are included in the species description of plants, the second set of words on the garden tag. Recognizing some of these will help you understand the character of the plants you see and purchase, and probably impress friends. Unfortunately these are a mere fraction of the species terms used . . . but this is a start and should be a great help. Don't be intimidated. Language is power.

Breaking the code

Look at this plant and read the botanical name. the clues are there. *Cedrus atlantica* 'Glauca Pendula.'

Weeping Blue Atlas Cedar

Genus is listed first, then species definers; then last is the particular variety or cultivar. This can signify place of origin or discovery, or the name of the

botanist who may have discovered or cultivated the plant. The suffix *ae* describes place of origin, *ii* signifies the particular botanist who named the plant.

Chamaecyparis obtusa 'Crippsii'

Here is a brief list—a few key Latin words to help in plant recognition and selection. These would appear as species or specific descriptors (adjectives). The genus is listed first: for example *Juniperus* (juniper) *horizontalis*. The species words (in this case, *horizontalis*) would be listed next, quite often more than one. Look at these words. See how descriptive they really are, and how easily translatable.

Take the first one. How far a stretch is *affinis* to *affinity*? The plant including this term in its name would be related (or have an affinity) to another plant, probably also listed in the name. How far a stretch *effusus* to *effusive*?

affinis	related to
albus or *alba*	white
alpinus	mountainous or of mountain climate
arborescens	becoming tree-like (in form)
atropurpureus	dark purple (usually foliage)
augustus	majestic
aurea or *aureus*	golden
coloratus	colored
contorta	contorted or twisted
declinatus	bent downward
deflexus	bent abruptly downward
densus	dense
edulis	edible
effusus	very loose, spreading
elegans	elegant
erectus	erect
excellens	excellent
excelsior	very tall
fragrans	fragrant
frigidis	of cold regions
fructifera	fruit bearing
giganteum	very big
glabrescens or *glabrous*	smoothish, often shiny
gracilis or *gracillimis*	graceful
grandiflorus	large-flowered
grandis	big
griseus	gray-colored
horizontalis	prostrate or horizontal in growth
herbaceous	not woody, herb-like
imperialis	royal or kingly
incisifolius	sharp, or cut-leaved
japonicus	Japanese
lacteus	milk white
lanceofolius	lance-like leaves
lavendula	lavender-like
magnificus	magnificent
magnus	large
mas or *masculatus*	male
maritimus	of the sea
melancholicus	hanging or drooping
nana or *nanalus*	dwarf or very dwarf
noctiflorus	night flowering
obtisatus or *obtusifolia*	blunt, obtuse
ovatus	ovate-leaved
pendula or *pendaflorus*	weeping, hanging flowers
perennis	perennial
petreus	rock loving
planus	flat plane
procumbens	procumbent, laying down
pygmea	very small
reniformis	kidney-shaped
robustus	robust
rosaflorus	rose-like flower
rubra or *rubescens*	red or becoming red
serpens	creeping, crawling, snake-like
sinicus or *sinensis*	Chinese
spectandrun or *spectabalis*	showy, spectacular
supinus	prostrate
sylvestris	of the woods
titanis	very large
tricolor	three-colored
tubatus	trumpet-shaped
umbracillifera	umbrella-shaped
undulafolius	twisted foliage

urbanis	city loving
vagans	wandering
vegetatus	vigorous growth
versicolor	various colors
verescens or *viridescens*	green or becoming green
viridis	green
vulgaris	common
zebrinas	striped

Again, this is just a very small sampling of species terms that will help you identify plants either in the nursery or the garden. I've listed those that are fairly easily translated to English. All plants can be identified in this way, so if this interests you I encourage you to continue your study of the Latin nomenclature of plants. It's pretty satisfying to be able to read the label on a plant, and understand its character from its name. And when you're trying to find something for a small space in your yard, it keeps you from purchasing a plant that includes in its name the word *giganteum*, I'm sure Linnaeus would be pleased, as will, no doubt, your spouse or whomever you share your humble plot with.

Now that you've begun to decipher the Linnaeus Code, here are some of the simple and universal characteristics of plants that you may want to understand to begin to use them as elements of design. Many of them will be familiar.

Hinoki Cypress

Understanding Plants as an Element of Design

Some plants have inherent architectural quality. Loosely interpreted to mean that the plant has interesting lines, compelling form or presence in and of itself. Besides celebrating the flower color and form, we need to acknowledge the plant itself.

BASIC IDENTIFYING TERMS

Evergreen: Retains its foliage through seasons. Can come in many shapes and forms.

Deciduous: Loses most or all of its foliage in a dormant season.

Coniferous: Bearing cones. A variety of plants in a variety of forms, usually evergreen.

Woody plants: Plants that develop thick or woody stems.

Herbaceous: Plants that are dominated in form and character by soft, leafy growth.

Annual: Flowers or plants that thrive for one growing season and then die off, sometimes leaving seeds that will begin the cycle again.

Perennial: Plants that come back every season, usually after a prolonged dormant period.

Biennial: plants that bloom for two years before dying off.

Ground covers: This term encompasses a variety of plants—perennials, evergreen, herbaceous—with the common characteristic that they don't develop any substantial height. They usually spread by underground roots or rhizomes across the ground, covering substantial area.

Grasses: Lawn grasses are single- or multiple-bladed plants that spread by root and rhizome. Some are annual, others perennial. The most successful lawns in varied climates consist of varied plant types—say, annual ryegrass, perennial rye, and Kentucky Bluegrass.

Ornamental Grasses: Plants cultivated for their particular form rather than as a ground cover or lawn crop. There is a large variety, with very distinct growth habits, from six inches to twelve feet or more. (*Miscanthus floridulus* 'giganteus' can have twelve-foot silver plumes.)

BASIC SHAPES

The association of elements is important to design. Think about how you combine plants and to what effect.

Pyramidal
or conical

Columnar

Globe

Vase

Prostrate

BASIC GROWTH HABITS

Prostrate: Lateral growth hugging the ground.

Ground cover: Spreading along the ground

Upright: A vertical element, narrow and distinct

Espalier: Growing attached to something else, a trellis or a chimney (usually trained or tied)

Weeping: Cascading foliage and or stem structure

Using growth habits to your advantage is a key to successful landscape design. Understand the changing nature of the plants and the changing nature of their relationship. Plants grow at different rates as well as with varied habits. The varied shapes and habits of plants can offer dynamic interest in the garden, integrating forms.

A FEW BASIC TEXTURES

Coarse needled: Usually short-needled evergreens like spruce.

Soft needled: Long-needled, such as pines.

Glossy leaved: Smooth and shiny-surfaced leaves, usually broadleaves like rhododendrons.

Waxy: Usually shiny-leaved with some residue

Succulent: Thick, usually water-filled foliage, like sedum.

Pubescent: A slight "hair" on the surface of the leaf, more visible in low sunlight.

Spiny: May infer an opened or twisted branch.

Fern-like: Usually opposite-leaved and sprawling.

There are many more . . . and you can make up your own if they enable you to see and define plants. Contrasting textures can be exciting in the garden. Too similar textures can often be quite confusing. Repeating varied textures often seems to offer the most compelling design.

Cedrus atlantica 'glauca': spiny and coarse

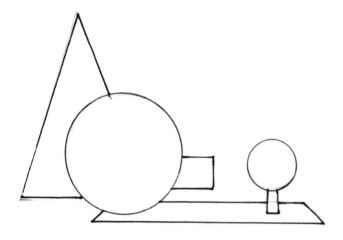

Texture combinations

Even placed randomly in the nursery, look at the variety of form and color.

51

Texture can translate to dramatic light and shadow.

Concrete, brick, and bluestone.

Pavers and plants.

Boulders and riverjack.

Stone and grass.

Plants and ornament.

". . . an imitation of nature"

The beauty of washed stone.

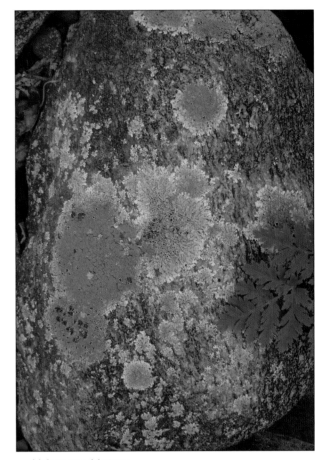

Lichen on old stone.

Birch bark.

Flowers and stone wall.

THE APPROACH
walkways and paths

On the old highway maps of America, the main routes were in red and the back roads blue. Now even those colors are changing. But in the brevities just before dawn and a little after dusk—the times neither day nor night—the old roads return to the sky some of its color."
—*William Least Heat Moon,* Blue Highways

The shortest distance between two points is a straight line. This is certainly true. But we all know this isn't always the most pleasant trip. Read *Blue Highways* by William Least Heat Moon. He traveled around the country along the secondary roads—the highways marked in blue on the road map—to discover the real America. It might not be too large a leap to say that a similarly considered alternative approach to your home can alter your perspective and appreciation. There's something to be said for meandering.

A common scenario: You're in a new home. You just had your first party, or another party that reminded you of the same problem. Nobody wants to come to the front door. These days everyone drives (except perhaps for crazy Uncle Walter) and your garage and driveway are off to the side, a world away from the front door. Perhaps the builder put in some stepping-stones or a narrow concrete slab that looks like a runway, but it's so uninviting that no one is drawn that way. The side door's closer. The garage entrance is more convenient. Because of this, no one ever really sees the front of your beautiful home. Well, it's time to do something about it. It's your castle . . . show it off.

Entrance walkways are keys to the *binding* of the exterior and interior of your home, and they control the approach of visitors. Your architect may have gone to great lengths to include an inviting foyer or wide front interior entrance hall. Unfortunately, the front landscape offers little transition to this wonderful feature of your home. Everyone comes through the mudroom or kitchen: So much for the architect's efforts. The failure is in the fact that the architect usually stops at the inside or outside walls. The rest of your home occurs just beyond that point. The landscape is often up to you.

Historically our entrance walks ran straight out to the sidewalk or road. This accommodated traditional pedestrian traffic. For better or worse, no one walks anymore, and even fewer ride a horse and carriage. Except for perhaps the mailman or the paper boy, no one approaches from the front of the house. And this is probably the best view of the home, across the front lawn or gardens. But the fact is, most guests arrive from the driveway. We simply need to find ways to manipulate their journey. And at its most effective, this manipulation will never be noticed.

The first thing most folks start to sweat over as they consider a walkway is what material to use for construction. What will be the surface of the walk? What will it look like? In fact, this is the last thing you should be thinking about. The first and most important thing to consider is the layout: the most comfortable, attractive, and inviting approach.

To begin figuring this, take a look at your yard. If there is no walk at all, where are the footprints that mark where people have walked? Where is the grass bent or worn out? If you were showing someone your house or if you were thinking of selling it—what approach would you take? Where would you pause to stand? What perspective best shows off the scale and architecture of the house? You probably wouldn't approach in a straight line parallel with the foundation. You probably wouldn't stand five or six feet from the foundation and gaze upward. You would step back. You would move away until the scale of the house reaches a more human proportion. A great many entrance walkways are five or six feet away from the house in straight line. This seems the most common mistake of front walks. The shortest route between two points may well be a straight line, but it's rarely the most interesting and never the most graceful.

Dogs know a good path.

Antique brick.

Bluestone.

THUMB NAIL SKETCH. ENTRANCE WALKWAY.

Walkway design: framing and focus

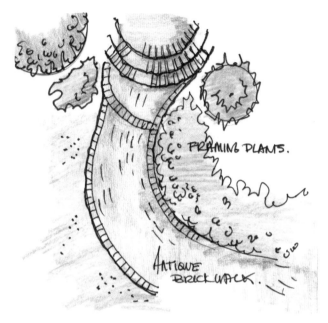

Once you've established a comfortable and inviting approach to the front door, you can begin to consider some other principles. Just as inside your home long hallways are often interrupted with open landings, if your walkway is long you may want to consider some outdoor landings. From many driveways, due to the architecture of the house, you can't even see the front door. This presents an even greater challenge. In this case consider a broad outdoor foyer, a landing that your eye can pick up so that the guest can see the destination. It's much more inviting this way. You might even consider a bench or a playful grouping of potted plants to attract attention. Statuary or artwork (whimsy is "in" in the gardening world) might mark the importance or focus of the main entrance. You do this inside all the time with furniture or featured artwork over the mantel. These same principles apply outside.

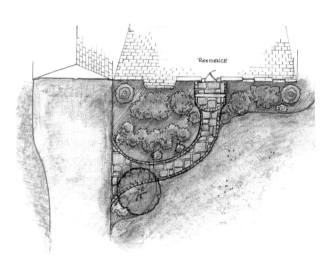

Find a comfortable approach, graceful lines, and a nice layout. Frame and soften with plants creating a focus at the destination.

Try to envision the finished landscape.

Plants soften the lines of an entrance walk.

Walkway Design

Plants might be the best way to draw the focus to the entrance. Framing the walkway appropriately with border plantings that grace the lines is a great way to direct traffic. A highly attractive or interesting "specimen" plant at the destination can create a visual focal point. Bright colors might draw your eye to the entry, just as a work of art or an accent piece might draw your eye from a hallway to a room inside. Try a weeping or cascading evergreen in the far garden. This might serve to both attract the eye toward it, and draw it back down to the walkway and entry.

There is no question where to walk on this secondary path.

Once you've agreed where the most inviting approach to your home should be, it's time to start sweating the details. Lay out a garden hose or spray-paint the grass where the natural traffic occurs. Experiment a little with simple curves. Make the walk wide enough so that two people can walk side by side (usually at least forty inches). Now you've imagined and designed a nice entrance to your home.

GARDEN PATHS

Scale is an important consideration. Usually a smaller scale walkway is appropriate for a path through a garden, whether formal or informal.

The full and active garden—that is, one that reflects all of the fun you're having experimenting with plants and color and growth habit—becomes by nature robust and full. Eventually it can become impenetrable, visually and physically, as well: so full with beautiful species of plants that it is difficult to walk through for enjoyment or cultivation. This calls for an access or garden path.

The view.

As practical as these might be these paths can be visual entries into and through the garden. The sight line might run through the garden bed to an alluring open space in the background, or it could resolve visually at a secondary garden, feeding that "excitement of the mind" that the author E. L Doctorow calls the beginning of the writing process for any book. Remember, my tenet is that all of these excitements are very much the same: *excitement affinis,* if you will.

A path changes the scale and access to the garden as well as creating depth.

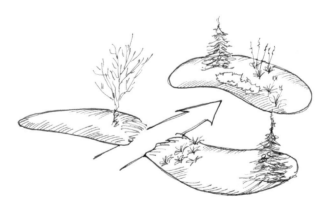

A viewing avenue can lead the eye to a secondary garden or space

Secondary paths

I refer to those landscapes where all the entries and spaces of the yard are connected with walkways as "Lionel Train set scapes." A complicated network of walkways and path connects all the dots: basement hatchway, pool gate, playscape, deck, patio, and so on. This is usually unnecessary and overdone. By creating too many walkways we take away from the primary paths on which we want to invite traffic. I strongly suggest resisting the impulse to connect all of the various entries and spaces of the yard. At times, open lawn can be the most inviting path and a perfect medium to walk across. With intricately designed and created spaces—like poolscapes or decks—the separation of lawn might be just the thing to simplify the image. Simpler is better. Still, if you must connect the spaces, don't always think in linear terms. Sometimes we need to visually slow down. Create some outdoor "foyers" where we can rest visually or even physically.

Path Materials

The materials that you can use for garden or secondary paths are nearly limitless. I tend to believe they should be less formal than those for an entrance walk. Simply take some of the *hard* out of *hardscape:* perhaps singular stepping-stones or flat fieldstones, slate or bluestone stepping-stones. Those with a slightly shattered look can give the garden a look of age even if it's fairly new. Crushed or washed stone or even a mulch path might be appropriate. The material depends on the garden size and scale. Usually, with a garden path, smaller is better.

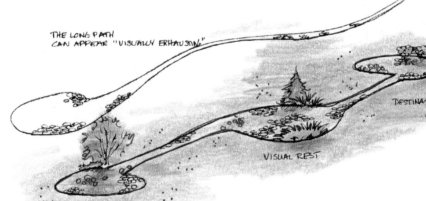

If you need to connect spaces over a long distance, it's often nice to break things up with landings, just as the hallways and connecting arteries of the house are subdued by foyers and open space.

In this photo, rather than connecting the dots with a long path I introduced a few steps and garden in the middle ground to visually connect two spaces quite removed from each other.

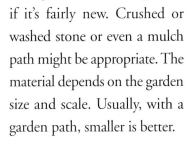

61

Secondary paths can be first class.

Casual stepping stones framed in hosta.

Natural stone has its own inherent beauty, derived from color, texture, and form.

These can be less formal than your primary entrances. Have some fun with them.

Ascending through gardens.

Old stone and moss can be perfect in a shady setting.

Path, garden, and stone bench combine to create a peaceful environment.

Here's one of my designs for connecting a gazebo to a driveway. Rather than a narrow path I decided to manipulate the space by widening the serpentine walk and using stone steps to achieve appropriate scale. Now the gazebo seems to fit or belong next to the larger structure of the house.

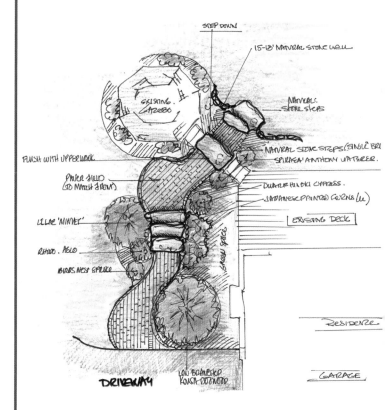

This is the stone that will form the steps, still in the quarry.

The stone wall and steps.

Excavation and preparation.

An outdoor "foyer."

The connecting path.

Keeping the path green is another approach. Either introduce or re-cover a path of lawn grass that meanders through or between gardens. These visual "avenues" can really change the scale of the garden and create more interest by creating more edges or borders. Allowing moss to develop in an open path can be beautifully simple and simply beautiful. The traditional approach—a combination of stepping-stones set into a bed of creeping thyme or sedums—can be a wonderful blend of greenscape and hardscape, serving as a binding element to the garden and its surroundings.

Grand Avenues

THE CRAFT

CONSTRUCTING WALKWAYS

Excavation: Although directly related to soil composition and grade, the excavation for a walkway should generally be eight to ten inches. Sandy soils may require less excavation, while clay-based soils may require more. This relates to the saturation point of the soil and its ability to freely absorb moisture. Excavate a straight-edged trench, allowing for four to six inches on either side (a total of eight to twelve inches for the entire width) of the anticipated width of the walkway. Excavate to a level base.

Preparation: For a base material, use either crushed stone or processed gravel to a third of the depth. This should be compacted with a plate compacter. Hand or manual compactors can be used for smaller areas. Filter fabric is suggested between layers of aggregate, but I've seldom found this to be necessary.

The finishing or top layer should be a fine particulate matter: masonry sand or stone dust. I've had great luck with stone dust, a pulverized rock that compacts to form a hard yet workable surface. It varies in graininess according to its source. Once you've achieved the elevation of the underlayment material (the desired surface height minus the thickness of your paving material), you should gently soak the material and compact it numerous times to create a fixed surface.

Final grade is critical. Final grade should represent the final grade (not the height) of the paving material with little or no adjustment. Once this grade is achieved, the field of pavers should go down quickly and without much calculation. Curving, intersecting, or cutting edges to the pavers is another step. Some pavers also have an integral pattern to follow. You can cut masonry wet or dry. Diamond-bladed saws are necessary to cut clean lines in stone or other paving products.

Remember pitch. You want to pitch the walkways away from the house foundation if it's an approach walkway. A pitch of 2 percent, which equates to less than a quarter inch per linear foot, is recommended. This means if you're constructing a walkway that will be four feet wide, it should pitch about an inch from one side to the other. This assures that water does not stand, but rather moves across the surface.

If the path you're constructing runs through a plane of lawn or garden that is level, the walkway should be crowned slightly in the middle so water sheds off both ways.

The material you choose matters less in this construction phase. There is great similarity to installing all the available paving material, from brick to flagstone. The advantages to manufactured paving materials are that they are generally dimensionally uniform, whereas natural field-, flag- or even bluestone may vary greatly in thickness. This makes the final prep and installation a bit more challenging. Each piece may need to be individually set while you're still concentrating and justifying the final walking surface.

Finishing: Once the paving element is laid, sweep fine dust or sand into the cracks (the spaces between the pavers). If you're using a concrete material, you can leave a fine layer of particulate material on the surface; and once you've secured the edges, use the compacter again to firm things up. If you're using a natural stone, this shouldn't be attempted—material might shatter. Your spacing will also be wider and varied and more filler will be required. But this is negative space and really part of the innate character of the material; it should be part of the beauty of the path.

In other words, the more natural or varied the paving material, the more we wander from the craft back to the realm of art.

GRAND ENTRANCES

The integration of the elements.

THE SPACE BETWEEN

Transitions: decks and porches

The rain that falls
Splash in your heart
Ran like sadness down the window into . . .
The space between . . .
—Dave Mathews

It's out there. You can see it from your chair in the kitchen. You have glimpses of it from the living room windows. It is either vast expanse of open lawn thirsting for water and fertilizer, or what is left of the trees on the fringe of the swath of land carved out for the construction of your house. It's either as flat as a landing pad or reminds you of a sloping Italian vineyard, useless for volleyball or having a catch or tossing a Frisbee with the kids. It's through the door, down a few wooden steps, or along the crooked concrete porch left by the last contractor on site. The space out

there and the one inside are separate and isolated from each other. They are distinct and not integrated at all.

In the new home, as the door closes behind you, you're left alone with it. Brown patches of lawn baking in the sun. A five-foot-high twisted growth that you are trying to convince yourself is a wildflower or a special plant that the builder left for you in some final gesture of kindness. It's got a swollen bud on it that appears ready to burst open into unimaginable beauty. There is a bulge of stone at your heel that you worry is the size of a buried Volkswagen. The kids are gathered at the window to see what you'll do to transform the yard for them. It is a separate place. They are all comfortably inside while you're out here in the vast and troubling unknown. The distance you have crossed seems strangely broad; the separation of the house from the yard, an abyss. You look back to the kids and they wave and smile. They are safe inside the home you have provided for them and you are way out in the yard, standing in the last frontier. The separation is glaringly vivid. It's one of the first problems to address.

Integration

In too many instances the transition of interior and exterior is awkward. Decks, porches, and patios seem to have evolved into poorly considered extensions slapped onto the back of houses or off the nearest slider. In fact, these are crucial connectors for living spaces. They should serve not only as additional space but as transitions, either drawing you outside with inviting lines and features, or allowing you to view and appreciate the house from a comfortable vista. Too often the elevated deck in particular, is a corralled space set out to accommodate the grill or a single table and chairs. On elevated decks, building code requirements force all kinds of railings that obscure the view and increase the separation of the spaces. Careful thought and planning will help make the deck not only a place for a barbecue or enjoying a summer meal, but the artery that connects the home to the living spaces of the yard. The deck or patio should contribute to the integration of these spaces.

Your yard is, or should be, an extension of your home. The outside space should be as inviting as the room at the end of the hallway inside the house. Think of the illuminated painting over the mantel: That wash of color and light draws you from one space to the next. In much the same manner, points of interest or focal points can draw you outside. The deck is a primary means of your liberation.

Layout and design are keys. There's nothing worse than spending a summer of Sundays building a wooden deck and then sitting down at the kitchen or dining room table, slapping open a beer or pouring a glass of iced tea, and looking out at nothing but railing spindles. You know it's well constructed. You dug

the footings yourself, leaving no stone (and you do mean *no stone*) unturned. You set the sonotubes (heavy cardboard columns that you insert into the ground and fill with concrete) yourself beyond the unholy depth of the frost. You used 2x8-inch frame, 16 inches on center. You used the best decking lumber you could find. You screwed each board down with galvanized or plastic-coated screws. But now, with your wife and the kids sitting at the table with you, it's all about the railing—because that's all you can see. The new flowering cherry tree is just out of sight. You can't see the garden you tilled last weekend. It's obscured by vertical spindles. Out of sight stretches the flat lawn and all its promise. But the spindles, those you can see. You can almost watch them begin to warp and check in the afternoon sun. And the sun itself is dispersed into stripes and bars that seem to follow you as you move. It's as if you've been corralled.

They won't say much. They know better than to mention it. And it's not uncommon. But it was your intention to build a beautiful and practical deck. And all you can see is the railing spindles.

THE UNFORTUNATE RAILING . . .   . . . THE LIBERATION

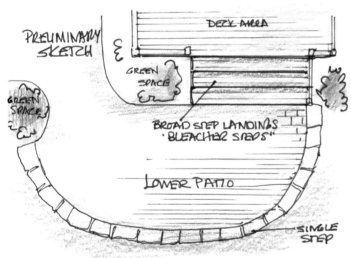

PRELIMINARY SKETCH

DECK AREA

GREEN SPACE

GREEN SPACE

BROAD STEP LANDINGS "BLEACHER STEPS"

LOWER PATIO

SINGLE STEP

Railings can often completely obscure the view turning the deck into a corral. The railing problem is a significant one. Besides giving the same attention you would allow the trim or details inside the house to the design and construction of the railing, one way to resolve the issue is to lay out the deck so that it allows for wide steps leading comfortably (and without thought about negotiating awkward stairs) toward the yard, opening up the sight line.

Sight lines are crucial: Here's a design sketch illustrating an uninterrupted view from the inside out.

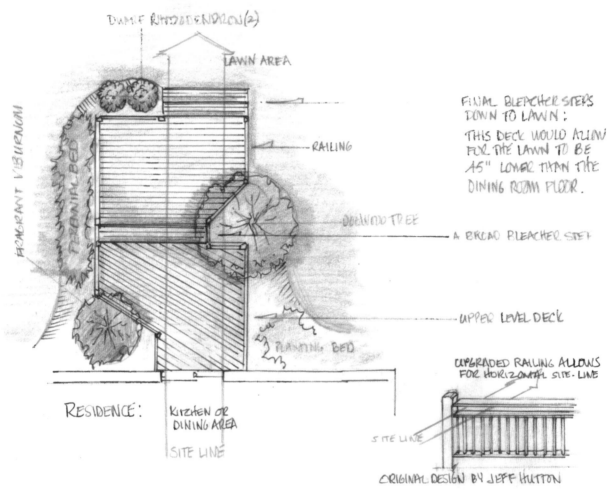

WOODEN DECK: BY MANIPULATING THE SHAPE AND DROPPING THE LEVELS, APPEALING SPACES ARE CREATED AND THE IMPORTANT SITE LINE (INSIDE OUT) IS LESS OBSCURED.

DWARF RHODODENDRON (2)

LAWN AREA

FRAGRANT VIBURNUM

RHODODENDRON BED

RAILING

DOGWOOD TREE

PLANTING BED

RESIDENCE: KITCHEN OR DINING AREA

SITE LINE

FINAL BLEACHER STEPS DOWN TO LAWN:
THIS DECK WOULD ALLOW FOR THE LAWN TO BE 45" LOWER THAN THE DINING ROOM FLOOR.

A BROAD BLEACHER STEP

UPPER LEVEL DECK

UPGRADED RAILING ALLOWS FOR HORIZONTAL SITE-LINE

SITE LINE

ORIGINAL DESIGN BY JEFF HUTTON

Before: the obstructed view line.

After: Liberated view. These steps will descend to a patio while an unobscured view is opened. This simple revision altered the space wonderfully.

This allows for creative railing treatments that might provide an uninterrupted view of the yard. By staging down with broad platforms, the sight line of the railing drops at seven-and-a-half-inch increments, normal for step risers (the vertical increments of a set of steps). This landing treatment can draw any railing completely out of the sight line. Sight lines are crucial to feeling comfortable and united, indoors and out. The ease of transition is critical to connecting the yard to the house and making all the space of your property an integral part of your home. And transitions begin visually. That first step is much more inviting if we have some destination in sight. Once the path is clear and inviting, the rest will follow. In fact, the placement of bold or hot-colored flowering plants (reds, bright yellows) or an interesting specimen shrub might act as a visual draw. The placement of potted plants can direct both the eye and traffic patterns. Once you've got the deck built, you can have fun decorating and manipulating furniture. A fragrant potted plant such as a rose can shield the space of the grill . . .

This is *your* baby. Remember the art. Before you limit yourself with practical considerations (lumber costs, degree of difficulty to build, et cetera), have some fun with the conception of what best suits the site and your lifestyle. The time for compromise is later. Now it's time to imagine.

Isn't that spatial? Conceive the shape and size

The deck shape itself need not be rectangular or square. It need not simply be attached to the back of the house. Experiment a little with the size and form of this element of your home. Place a seat where you feel the most comfortable in relation to the house. I think you'll find this will be at least six to ten feet away. All that deck space against the walls of the house isn't particularly inviting. Most decks seem to imagine us with our back to the rear siding and the open yard in front of us: sort of a defensive posture to design, as if we're guarding the homestead from invaders. Push away from the wall. Get to a place where you're comfortably removed from the siding and at least somewhat inserted into the space of the rear yard. As we did with the front walkway, find the perspective that makes the form or architecture of the house the most inviting . . . the relationship of the shapes somewhat balanced. Try placing a bunch of chairs out where you feel the most comfortable and adjust them until you decide that this is the right spot. Stand where you might stand to take a picture of the house (a close-up, but not a detail of the fading vinyl siding). Now begin the design of your deck. Find a way to get to that comfortable outdoor space.

There are practical considerations, but try to see beyond the most practical and boring. The traditional square of wood may be the easiest to build— but take a minute to think. Do you really want to be near the crank-out window or a few feet from the dryer exhaust? Do you want your kids or your guests leaning against the siding or the on the sill of the window? Most likely you don't. So find the destination and figure out how to get there. One way to accomplish this is to create a small transition deck (an outdoor hallway) from the door that opens up to a broader space more removed from the house.

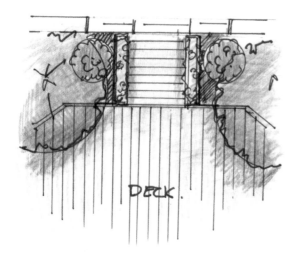

DINING ROOM

DECK.

Introduce greenspace.

This will afford you the opportunity to put some greenspace between the deck area and the structure of the house, softening all the architectural lines and creating a feeling that you're actually removed and in a separate and distinct space. Plants can offer some shade, fragrance, and the soft texture of flower and foliage. Heavy foliage can even absorb noise or the harshness of certain sounds. Try some of the smaller lilacs like *Syringa palibiniana* 'Meyeri' or 'Miss Kim'. Many of the viburnums offer beautiful flower and fragrance. Try *Viburnum carlesii. Clethra paniculata* or improved sweet pepper bush is wonderfully fragrant and simple, not a focus but a transition plant. If you want a more architectural element or a permanent screen, look at dwarf evergreens such as *Chamaecyparis obtusa* 'Nana Hinoki' or the many others available in the nursery marketplace. Go to the garden centers armed with your "species cheat list" and have some fun picking out just the right plant for the space. Remember, we've already broken some of the Linneaus Code.

There are considerable advantages to moving away from the edges of the indoor space. You've taken the barbecue with you, and the smoke won't be trapped under the eaves of the house as it might have been. The water from the roof doesn't drip into your cocktail. And you're out there. You're into the back forty. The deck is no longer a thing between the inside and outside of the house, but rather a binding element that brings it together. It extends your living space into the yard and integrates the inside and outside, both visually and practically. When you're out there you're still connected to everything inside, but you're somewhat removed. I understand that there are times when you might not want to be connected at all, and for this you can create a variety of detached outdoor rooms beyond the transition space. (See the chapter called "Open to the Sky").

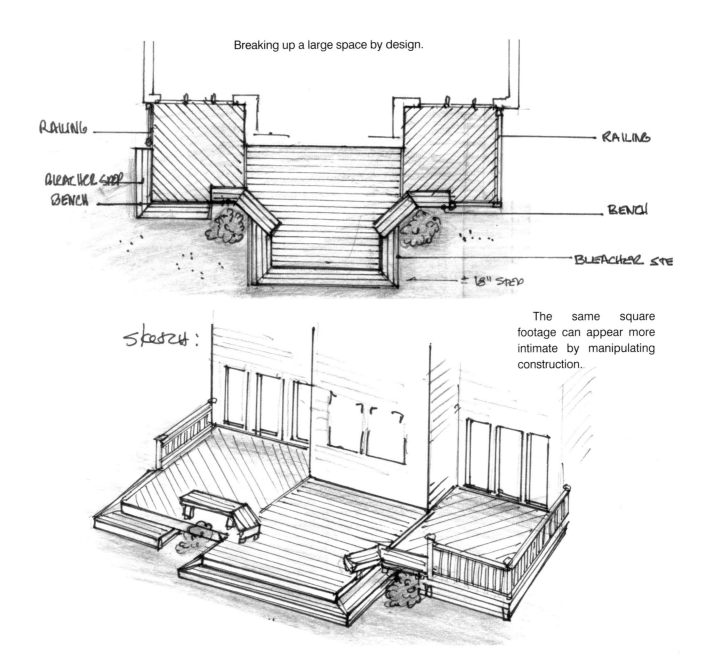

Breaking up a large space by design.

RAILING

BLEACHER STEP
BENCH

RAILING

BENCH

BLEACHER STE

± 18" STEP

Sketch:

The same square footage can appear more intimate by manipulating construction.

The scale of the deck or the perception of size can be altered by the details of design and construction. Just as molding or a wainscot can alter the scale of an interior room, there are many ways to manipulate the scale of an outdoor deck or patio.

Okay. You've carefully considered the space and the spatial relationships. You've designed a deck that that accommodates your needs and desires. If you feel

capable, prepare a simple sketch or scale drawing. Measure the width and length and delineate the exact shape you would like. If you intend to hire a professional to build your deck, you now have a good idea of exactly what you want. Most professionals can take your ideas and translate them into a nice reality. And if you're going to build it yourself, well, you're ready to sweat the details.

THE CRAFT

BASIC DECK CONSTRUCTION

Before beginning any construction project, consult your local building codes. A wooden deck is a structure that has engineering requirements, and you should have basic construction knowledge. This is simply meant to be a quick reference, a checklist.

After you've designed the new deck or consulted with a designer, determine the desired height of your finished deck and the thickness of the decking material you've chosen, and work your way down through this support material. By doing this you'll arrive at the appropriate height of the different layers of support.

Foundations: Basically, raised wooden decks are constructed on footings or posts. These need to be submerged in the ground under the local level of frost. This depth varies with the climate you're building in as well as soil conditions. The number of posts you'll need varies as well, with size and height from the ground.

Concrete footings are generally recommended. These can be dug and poured in readily available cardboard forms; the required diameter of these footings also varies by construction and conditions. As they emerge from the ground at the designated height, vertical support posts (wooden 4x4s or 6x6s) are mounted on top of them to the height of carrier beams. There are composite plates that separate wood from concrete required in many circumstances. There are cases where steel posts may substitute for wood.

The size and thickness of carrier beams is directly related to the span of construction they support. Double 2x8 or even triple 2x10 might be required to support the deck you've designed. This is also directly related to the number of footings installed. Fewer footings dictate longer spans to support, therefore requiring sturdier construction.

Connect to the house: A ledger board (a mounting board where the deck connects to the house, if it will) is generally a 2x8 or 2x10 mounted with bolts to the house wall at the height of the framing. The top of the ledger will be level with the top of the anticipated framing. With exceptions, the framing or joists are usually standard sixteen inches on center and constructed just below the decking (or floor) surface, perpendicular to the ledger and the carrier beams. Again, depending on specific site and design, these can be 2x6 or 2x8. The center of each framing board is mounted sixteen inches from the center of the next. Metal joist hangers are used at the ends, mounting the framing to the ledger.

Note: Some composite decking requires tighter, more frequent framing layout.

Frame and surface: The finished frame rests on the carrier beams which distribute and support the anticipated weight. Often, the framing of exterior decks is weather-resistant, such as "pressure-treated" lumber. This is wood that has been treated with preservative under pressure to resist the elements of climate. There is other lumber that is naturally weather-resistant.

Cedar, redwood, mahogany, and many other woods are appropriate for the deck surface. All have their pluses and minuses. There are a great variety of composite materials available in the marketplace that are durable and long lasting. Any wood exposed to the elements changes over time, which is why composite material has found increasing popularity. The aesthetic judgment is up to the homeowner/designer.

Railing systems are a key to the construction and look of the new deck. Railings are necessary on most decks. There are lower decks (twenty-four inches from grade for instance) that may not require railings. The height may vary with your local building codes so you need to check. There are specific requirements for distance between pickets or dowels, specific requirements regarding "grippability" on step railings, and more. Design is very important in this regard. Think about viewpoints and transitions. How can the impact of the railing be minimized? How can the views remain open?

Steps and the required railings can be the least pleasant part of the structure if not conceived properly. Try to avoid long spans that look like attic steps. This can be at times avoided by creating landings. Wide, bleacher-like steps may be an answer for lower decks.

Remember, wooden decks are considered construction and are subject to all the usual building requirements and codes. In this sense, they are truly outdoor rooms. The key is to imagine them this way. They are a transition from the indoors to the yard: a means as well as an end. Appropriately designed and constructed, they are at once a destination and a connection to the outdoor space of your home.

TRANSITIONS: The Space Between

OPEN TO THE SKY

Patios and courtyards

In the creation of the garden, the architect invites the partnership of the kingdom of nature. In a beautiful garden the majesty of nature is ever present, but it is nature reduced to human proportions and this transforms into the most efficient haven against the aggressiveness of contemporary life.

—Luis Barragán, architect

I am convinced that some of humanity's great work has been imagined and nourished while sitting in the secluded corner of a quiet patio, the fragrance of lilac swimming beneath the breeze, insects bouncing at the leaves of the hedge, the uncut grass bending. I may be wrong, and of course much too romantic, but the point here is that properly situated and executed, the patio or courtyard can be a quiet and enlightening space: an outdoor room, secluded yet part of the grand design of the landscape. A space of transition from world to world. The perfect partnership, "nature reduced to human proportions . . ."

Location. Location. Location.

That's always something to consider, and when it comes to this new outdoor space the location relative to the house is the first question to ponder. Are we creating this space to feel like an extension of the indoors? Do we want it to be close and convenient? Or are we trying to create a space separate and removed? Do we want a private space where we can be removed from the kids? Or are we trying to create a space for the kids so they can be removed from us? Do we want to be able to see the space from the house or do we want removed from view? All of these things can be accomplished and provide quite different results. Just as we plan a room indoors for a specific use and mood, we plan outdoor spaces.

The term and concept of our *patios* originate from the Spanish. Historically these were interior courtyards open to the sky, sometimes a central area surrounded by the structure of the house, or often a series of entries. In warmer climates, we pass though entrance spaces that are not clearly defined as inside and out. The warm, dry climate allows a beautiful exchange of light and space, in some cases the absence of the necessity for screens, and a wonderful symbiosis of the interior and exterior environment. The bright colors reflect the presence and exchange of sunlight as much as any different attitude toward the integration of inside and out.

Patios, those level spaces usually constructed of stone, brick, or some other kind of paving material, serve as one of our primary outdoor entertaining spaces. They can extend your living space and the enjoyment and value of your home. With little thought they are quite often simply squares or rectangles of open area attached to the rear of the house. Many times they can't even be seen from inside the house. If they are constructed off the rear wall, much of the space is uncomfortable and ends up being used for storage. Before creating another square of paving material in another backyard, consider the relationship the outdoor space has with the interior. Check the view from the kitchen or dining room. What do you see and where do you begin to see it?

Patio design

Study the space carefully before you do anything, from a variety of vistas. Place some stakes in the ground where your view truly begins from inside, a view not obscured by any structure of the house. Study the forms and color in the forefront (in the interior) and begin to extend that vision to the background space—which in this case happens to be outside. Is there a spot where you wish your view to come to a rest? Is there some form that should serve as a focal point or a visual anchor? Is this a big area in a small yard or a small area in a huge space? This is an important phase in the realization of your patio. The actual material—brick or stone or pavers—is not under consideration yet. Think first of how you want to manipulate the space and extend the living area of your home. See if your imagination allows you to see through the walls so you can effectively integrate the environment outside with your more familiar inside space. For the moment, forget winter and enjoy the season.

Sometimes the placement of an ornamental tree can help you imagine the space the patio should fill. By beginning to frame the area, and effectively alter the scale, you can begin to see the space as an outdoor room. A "ceiling" can be suggested with the canopy of a tree or a structure like an arbor or pergola, drawing your eye down—effectively collecting your vision. The perspective can be completely altered with the arrangement of associated elements: plants, garden shapes, visual features. A stone wall for framing or sitting can provide an outdoor wall or partition, just as has been achieved inside. The material you decide to use for the "floor" is important most of all as it relates to scale. We are quite lucky to have beautiful stone, sometimes called flagstone or garden path stone, available in New England; this can create a unique and ageless surface full of indigenous character and beauty. Clay brick is available and offers that cool, old-fashioned look of a garden patio. Bluestone is a large, quite bold natural material that forms a surface like large tile and can mimic interior surfaces. Concrete pavers are an evolving medium that are increasingly popular and come in a huge variety of style and color. But size matters. Smaller pavers can create a beautifully intricate look and style. Large bluestone can be bold and elegant. Natural fieldstone has that rugged and timeless look often associated with New England. However, all of these considerations pale in comparison with the placement, size, and shape of the patio.

Experiment on paper and on the ground, staking or painting. Remember "the Landscaper Theory of Relativity."

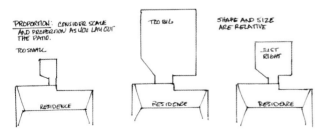

The "Goldilocks" approach: too small, too big, just right

By staking the space you can live in the area for a while before you start digging. Line out the shape with spray paint or a garden hose (use the garden hose on a hot day when it's easily pliable). Try introducing plants (greenspace) between the house and the edge of the patio. This gets you away from the siding or shingles while softening structure and line. Are there views that might need screening, either with structure or shrubs? As your patio moves away, following your sight line from inside, it more effectively becomes an extension of your living space. If you can see it and it bears some characteristics of the interior in either shape, scale, color, or character— you've effectively integrated the spaces. You've created a visual passage, just as the Spaniards created physical passages and rooms that were truly "inside out."

Imagine the use, the potential furniture you might be trying to accommodate. Will it be round or square, for instance?

Once the form is realized and the patio is installed, either professionally or by your own dedicated effort, you can continue integrating the spaces. Use similar accents: potted plants or simple statuary both inside and out in the adjacent spaces. Repeat color with flowers or appointments in related spaces.

Whimsy is "in" in landscaping. Have some fun with outdoor art or sculpture; be creative, showing some real enjoyment of outdoor spaces. You use plenty of art inside—use some outside as well. A wide variety of outdoor furniture is available in the market, from playful to elegant. Consider your interior look as you choose an appropriate exterior counterpart. Most of us don't have a climate that allows for a true interior courtyard "open to the sky," but we can manipulate the separation so the spaces feel connected.

As much as these new areas are wonderful for entertaining and relaxing, they are also key transition spaces from the inside to outside and vice versa. Create forms and shapes that are inviting. Create lines that connect you to the yard and don't stop your eye at the borders of the patio. Integrate your spaces by considering design long before you put a shovel in the ground. And most important, have some fun with the idea and its realization. Remember your wildest dreams.

Size and scale

Much has been made and much has been written about the concept of outdoor rooms. What this usually means is a reduced scale, either real or simply a feeling of privacy. To understand scale in this application I've often used the following example. (Although this does not come from my personal experience, in my younger days, I had many experiences similar to this one.)

You are being punished by a high school teacher. You're forced to sit in the center of the large gymnasium and read a book to which you were assigned but failed to finish. Sitting alone in the middle of this vast space, it is im-

possible to concentrate. Furthermore, your sense of self is diminished. The scale of things is wrong. A friendly custodian notices your dilemma. He goes to the storage closet and pulls out a rolling partition, which also serves as a blackboard. He rolls it to your side, nods in a friendly fashion, and walks away.

You look back to the page at which you've been staring for ten minutes and suddenly you begin to read. You haven't moved. You are still alone in the middle of the gym. But the presence of the partition has reduced the scale of the space. There is even a shadow cast across the floor and you can sense its edges. Your sense of self is elevated. Of course you'll read the book. You'll finish this afternoon. The space you occupy is now "human scale."

What changed? It's the same book and the same gymnasium. But the scale of the spaces has been greatly modified and your comfort level increased. The custodian understood this.

Space and scale can be easily manipulated outside. If you have a wide-open property, the placement of trees and shrubs is crucial to the manipulation of scale. If you have a wooded property, opening up some of the canopy might be appropriate: Carve out viewing avenues. Create visual paths. Replacing evergreens with deciduous plants in the forefront might help. Create the illusion of depth with the layering of plant heights and overall sizes (as discussed in other chapters), staging up from ground cover in the forefront to larger plant material in the back.

Scaling down is simpler. With the same knowledge displayed by the custodian in the gym, we can create appropriately scaled spaces in a large wide-open yard.

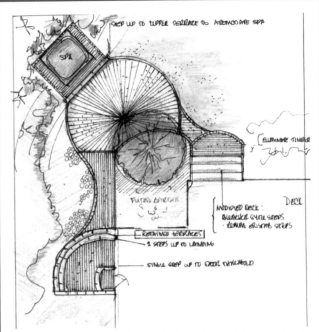

Here's a layout and the realization of a multi-terraced patio area. The primary interest lies in the line and form of the patios, allowing inviting transition, appropriate scale for a large property, and room for framing gardens.

CONSTRUCTING PATIOS

Excavation: Refer to the excavation suggestions for walkways, as many of the same requirements occur with the patio. Because of the broader exposure of the field of the patio, even more attention should be paid to grading and pitch. With more exposure and surface, there is simply more room for error.

Once again excavate a shape that accords with your design, and increase the excavation by six inches on all sides. This allows for backfill and securing the edge with either base material, topsoil graded appropriately, or some form of artificial edge.

Preparation: The base material should be a larger crushed aggregate. The larger material increases the drainage capacity. All layers of base material should be compacted with a plate compacter or by other means available. There are handheld tampers that are available and effective, but they mean a lot of manual labor.

Finishing: Again, the finishing or top layer should be a fine particulate matter: masonry sand or stone dust. These materials are sometimes called simply fines.

Pitch is even more critical for the broad field of a patio. You may need to establish multiple pitches over a large surface and varied grade. Keep in mind that you do not want water to stand on any area of the patio. Although professionals use a leveling transit to check specific grades, you might get away with a line level or a four-foot level . . . or both. Before you start laying the paving material, soak the fine dust again and see if there's any specific pooling of water. You can correct this fairly easily by adding or subtracting material.

If you're constructing a patio on a fairly level plane, you may need to crown the center so that water sheds off on all sides. This pitch should be subtle (no more than 2 percent).

Form and function: Whatever paving material you choose, remember to create compelling lines and form that provide enough space to accomplish your goals but not so much that you've created a form too large for the site. It's easier to manipulate the shape before you install any pavers, so it might be good to live with the excavation for a few days—viewing it from several angles or vistas and making sure your furniture, grill, and so on all fit appropriately.

OPEN TO THE SKY

There was music from my neighbor's house through the summer nights. In his blue gardens men and girls came and went like moths among the whisperings and the champagne and the stars.

—*F. Scott Fitzgerald,* The Great Gatsby

Inside out.

A thread of bluestone runs through a field of antique brick.

LAUREL POINT

Envision your patio as a room "open to the sky"—an integral part of your outdoor home.

THE AGONY AND THE ECSTASY

Gardening with perennials

In my experience, no gardening gets the gardener—novice or veteran—more excited, or the homeowner more interested in being considered a "gardener," than perennial gardening. Fraught with frustrations and the wonderful joy of error, the product of our efforts, great or small, can be exhilarating. When some people talk of gardening, this is what they're referring to. Claude Monet's famous gardens, the ageless impression saved for us on his canvases, consist primarily of masses of perennials. (Don't think *nonmaintenance*. Claude Monet had his grounds-keeper shine the lily pads in the pond every morning before he painted.) When I give talks to garden clubs and other groups, this is the topic in which they're most interested. Perhaps because of this, there are hundreds of wonderful books on perennials and perennial gardening. My own shelves are filled with them. But this is not one. I'll discuss perennials as an important element of the landscape, perhaps even a feature—but not more important than the whole.

Perennials can be used as a forefront to a garden of shrubs. They can form a garden path. They can be a focal point to the landscape.

There is, I believe, a thin line between the blooming perennial and the wildflower or weed. Perception is often the key. Another is control. Will the plant stay in one place or spread mercilessly across the garden and yard? Will it reseed itself at will? In fact, many species will do just that. These are usually excluded from the world of residential perennial flowers. Many marginal ones sneak into the market. Others have been brought into the "civilized" world (no longer wild)—they're wildflowers brought under control or cultivated to be appropriate to the garden: tamed, if you will. Sort of like having a beautiful wolf living in the backyard: There is always that slight fear that he might hear the "call."

I think we have to maintain a sense of humor as well as the sense of awe that remains with any successful perennial gardener. There is a sense of excitement and daring (well, maybe that's a little over the top—but it is a gamble every time out) inherent in gardening with perennial flowers. However, particularly with this experience, we might discover that symbiosis of art and nature. We might be humbled by our poor efforts in the face of powerful nature. And we might discover as well the wolf sleeping by the back door.

A few of the wolves in sheep's clothing

There are many perennials and ground covers that can *get wild*. These are great plants that can tend to be a little much. But controlling them can be done through root division and transplanting. In the old days these were shared with neighbors. It's probably still a great idea. Even with this downside, many are among my favorites. Here are a few of my favorite perennials, used often in the landscape, which have an inherent wild side.

Rudbeckia 'Goldsturm' (Black-eyed Susans): One of my favorite perennials for its showy yellow daisy flowers that linger well into fall, this plant can be overly aggressive and fill a small space quickly. Use it at borders in full sun or as wave of color in a large space.

Ajuga (carpet bugle): there are a lot of forms of this ground cover plant. Many are quite beautiful and provide a glossy foliage as a forefront or an aggressive ground cover for a large sunny area. But they can spread and reseed into the lawn.

Pachysandra terminalis (pachysandra or Japanese spurge): When in doubt, set pachysandra out. This dense evergreen mound spreads underground by stolon. It's wonderful for large shady areas where nothing else will grow but once it's established it hates to leave. Give it some room and let it do its thing.

Hemerocallis (daylily): This is simply a great summer perennial; many varieties bloom all summer and into early fall. But they are self-perpetuating and can cover some ground. Think *large borders* or *beds*. At times they can seem like the charming guest who stays a bit too late.

Iris sibirica (Siberian iris): Beautiful blooms in spring on a nicely architectural blade of a leaf. The multi-petaled flowers (blue, violet, white, and more) peer nicely over shrubs or other flowers. But they want to spread, and a single plant can become a four-foot-wide mass.

Use these plants liberally in the right spot. But give them room, or be prepared to divide the roots and spread the wealth of color to other areas . . . or other yards.

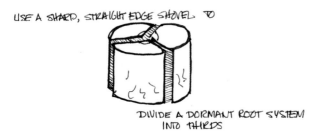

USE A SHARP, STRAIGHT EDGE SHOVEL TO

DIVIDE A DORMANT ROOT SYSTEM INTO THIRDS

Creating the garden

As with all gardening, the shape of the garden is very important. Remember, landscape is about the association of efforts. If perennials are the element you're using to create your visual display, then the edge and the shape are the frame of your art. Once again, try staking the space or painting lines, laying out the garden hose until you've got a pleasing shape that fits with the rest of the landscape. (Remember the "Theory of Relativity.") Start small rather than big. It's usually easier to expand a perennial garden than to shrink it.

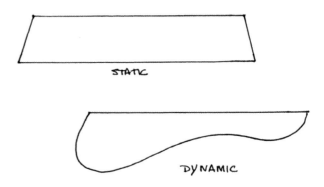

STATIC

DYNAMIC

With obvious exceptions, curves in the garden shape are usually the best complement to plant shapes. Otherwise you'll be trying to fit a round peg into a square hole, so to speak.

The view: Is the garden going to be seen from all sides (360 degrees), or only from one or two directions? Is it a forefront of other larger shrubs or trees? Is it a border garden along a path? Will you plant it for fragrance? To attract wildlife, such as butterflies? Is it seen close up, or from a distance? These are all important design considerations. The actual plants will be chosen out of careful consideration of color, size, mass, leaf, fragrance, period of bloom, and so forth. But as you establish these plants make yourself aware of their growth habit and the nature of their blossom. You're filling in spaces of a blank canvas. Refer to one of the many books on perennials, to the internet, or to the professional who can help you wade through the myriad choices. But I will say this: Anyone who says they've never made a mistake with perennials is self-deluded or a liar. There are so many plants available, with so many varied habits—it's easy to make a mistake. Sometime the mistakes are a delight. Sometime they're really annoying. But get over it. If you've laid out a nice bed and are working with a cool sun at your back, well, what can really go wrong?

Avoiding the temptation of filling these pages with beautiful photos of flowers, here are sketches and descriptions of just a few of my favorites. All are fairly easy to cultivate and care for.

THIRTY SIMPLE FAVORITES

ACHILLEA MILLEFOLIUM
'YARROW'

Achillea (yarrow): Almost a wildflower, perennial yarrow is a vigorous spreading plant with an intricate foliage (millefolium) structure that can create a lot of interest on its own. The small flower heads cover the plant in summer and can make a nice statement planted en masse or along a woodland border. Light shade or sun.

ANTHEMIS 'GOLDEN MARGUERITE'

Anthemis (golden Marguerite): Varieties of this daisy-like yellow flower boom in full sun from summer though fall. From six inches to two feet tall, they have a beautiful presence in any garden and can work as potted plants for single seasons.

Aquilegia (columbine): Native to Colorado in their wildest form, the hybrids are distinct, architectural flowers with colors from purple to deep pink. Plant in cool sun or partial shade and rich soil. In good conditions these plants will bloom from May to July, providing subtle color accent in the woodland or other shady garden.

ARMERIA MARATINA 'SEA PINK'

Armeria (sea pinks): This species presents small, dense flower heads clustered on tops of grassy foliage that can range in color from green to silver. The presence of the flower over the tufts of linear foliage is one of the plant's best assets. The other is its tolerance of poor soil conditions. Use by massing for borders or in rock gardens.

A STILBE 'False Spiraea'

Astilbe: (false spiraea) A flowering perennial tolerant of significant shade or nearly full sun, this is a relatively easy plant for the beginner. Its fern-like foliage has a great presence in the garden through the growing season, sending up plumes of flowers in mid- to late summer. A variety of colors and sizes are available: from towering white to short pink spikes.

ASTER × FRIKARTII

Aster: A neglect-tolerant daisy ranging in height from ten to thirty inches and more. In full sun to light shade they bloom in mid- to late summer and well into the fall. Mix varieties for dramatic effect and length of blooming season.

CAMPANULA CARPATICA

DELPHINIUM · BELLADONNA ·

Campanula (bell flower): A varied species, the "carpet" varieties (*carpatica*) form a low mound of tight foliage and present flowers most of the summer. Blue, white, or pink, they form a beautiful border or forefront to a sunny garden. The mature height of these doesn't exceed ten to twelve inches.

Delphinium: A beautiful, distinct blossom carried on an elegant stem. An "English garden" plant in the traditional sense, there are hundreds of varieties ranging from ten inches tall to seven feet tall, so be careful with your selection.

COREOPSIS VERTICILLATA
'MOONBEAM'

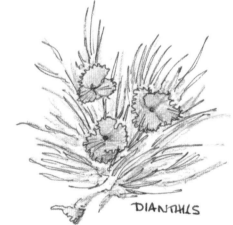

DIANTHUS

Coreopsis (Tickseed): Sporting an uncompelling name, varieties of this species are some of the great reliable plants for the summer garden. Dominated by yellow, there are varieties of pink and purple. The yellow wins out. *Coreopsis verticillata* 'Moonbeam' is one of the most reliable perennials for the beginning gardener. With full sun and decent soil the plant will bloom from June to October atop basal mounds of intricate foliage. 'Moonbeam' is a vigorous spreader, so be prepared to divide and conquer.

Dianthus (border pinks or carnations): These compact plants vary in foliage and flower and can form a beautiful border. In the right conditions (they prefer sweet, well-drained soil) the foliage is as attractive as the flowers, which range from white to magenta and most shades in between.

101

DICENTRA 'KIND OF HEARTS'

Dicentra (bleeding-heart): More common is the old-fashioned bleeding-heart, which puts on a dramatic show in April and then fades quickly. These new hybrids are continuous-bloom, sun-loving perennials with the same heart-shaped blossoms in many shades of pink and white. The foliage has nice detail and forms a neat clump, a nice accent in the forefront of a sunny garden.

ERIGERON 'PROSPERITY'

Erigeron (fleabane): A daisy resembling an aster with narrow rays or petals. In colors from lilac and lavender to pink, they thrive in sun, somewhat protected from the coldest weather. They range in height from ten inches to two feet. 'Prosperity' is a hardy, eighteen-inch lavender-blue variety.

ECHINACEA PURPUREA 'WHITE SWAN'

Echinacea (coneflower): As well known for its medicinal power as for its flowers, this is a dependable beauty in the sunny garden. Another daisy, its blooms range from purple to pink to white, with large dark center cones. From one to three feet in height, they bloom in late summer. Use as a centering plant or an accent in the large garden.

GALLARDIA 'GOBLIN' BLANKET FLOWER

Gaillardia (blanket flower): Perennial daisies indigenous to the Rocky Mountains, these are low-maintenance and dependable. There are many forms ranging from ten to thirty inches in height. The form I've sketched is 'Goblin', which combines the red and yellow range of colors of the species.

GERANIUM 'CRANESBILL'
'ANN FOLKARD'

Geranium (cranesbill) (*G. pretense*): A bright pink, nearly magenta blossom on a sprawling plant about eighteen inches high, it blooms in early to midsummer and spreads. Full sun to light shade.

HELIOPSIS   'SUNFLOWER'

Heliopsis (sunflower): One of the great standard daisies, helipopsis is an orange sunflower with forms from five inches to five feet, that thrive in the sunny garden.

HEMEROCALLIS "DAY LILY."

Hemerocallis: Daylilies are one of the most dependable flowers for the low-maintenance landscape. There are more forms and colors than I can mention in this context. Look to this plant for naturalizing along borders and as a natural mass of color. Many forms will bloom intermittently all summer and into early fall.

HEUCHERA

Heuchera: Common coral bells is just one familiar variety of this multifaceted perennial. I use it for its distinct and varied foliage, from bronze to silver to deep green. Heuchera also have handsome blossoms, generally on long, sturdy stems, but these are foliage plants that can make a beautiful statement when planted en masse, or as a backdrop for white or blue blossoms or contrasted with silver-foliage plants.

IRIS

HOSTA

Hosta: I couldn't leave this plant out. There are literally thousands of varieties of this perennial, most of them known for their distinct foliage and shade tolerance. Truly the aristocrat of the shade garden, these plants have their own society, with new varieties introduced every year. These are not your parents' hostas. Try combining some of the subtle foliage variations.

Iris: Few flowers bloom more beautifully or distinctly than the many varieties of iris. Bearded iris (*I.* x *germanica*) are usually less than thirty-six inches tall. There are Japanese Iris and Siberian Iris, all supported on a distinct sword-like foliage that gives high visibility in any garden. Blooming period varies from late spring to summer. Most do well in pretty good sun. They need some work; beginners might do best trying varieties of Siberian iris.

LEUCANTHEMUM 'SHASTA DAISIES'

Leucanthemum (Shasta daisy): Beautiful white daisies with yellow centers, these bloom mid- to late summer in forms that range in height from eight inches to four feet. Fairly vigorous in their spreading habit, they can fill a lot of space as a backdrop or a foil to brightly colored blossoms.

MONARDA Bergamot

Monarda (bee balm): With many hybrids from scarlet to violet and even white, these are beautiful additions to any garden. Many bloom all summer and do attract bees. Some plants fare better with occasional root division to avoid sprawl. Heights range from thirty inches to five feet and all prefer sun.

LOBELIA CARDINALIS.

Lobelia (cardinal flower): From deep red to clear blue, these bloom along upright stems atop clumps of foliage. Lobelias don't last too many years in the garden, but seem worth the effort. They range in height from twenty inches to three feet.

Paeonia (peony): Given their wide variety in color and height, these beautiful flowering perennials have a place in any feature garden. The absolute beauty of the blossom makes up for their very short blooming period. Most bloom in early summer and leave a nice foliage for the remainder. When in bloom they'll be the focal point of most gardens.

Perovskia (Russian sage): Distinct silver foliage and blooms that are a striking "almost blue" combine to make this a great plant. 'Little Spires' is a good sturdy variety that won't flop over; it matures at about twenty-four inches. This is a great mass planting or a foil for pinks, lavenders, blues, and purples.

Phlox: There are many forms of this plant with a great deal of variation. Some of the summer phlox are upright and distinct, while the form *p. subulata* is a mounding ground cover, blooming in early spring. All varieties are worthy of any garden and have particular uses and varied blooming periods. Some forms are susceptible to mildew problems and will have to be treated. For the most part, you should have phlox in some form in your landscape gardens.

RUDBECKIA 'Black eyed Susan'

Rudbeckia (coneflower): A common and very dependable staple of the summer garden. Varieties range in height and vigor of growth, but all sport the yellow daisy and a distinct center. Rudbeckia thrives with little or no maintenance and ranges in height from thirty inches to four feet. The variety 'Gold-strum' is best known as black-eyed Susan.

SALVIA

Salvia (sage): Species within this genus vary greatly but offer a similar flower head and graceful habit. The upright blooms are a wonderful accent, some almost blue in color, most in midsummer. Heights range from eight inches to three feet. All prefer full sun. Culinary sage, the common herb, is quite easy to grow. Mildew can be a problem and should be monitored.

SEDUM

Sedum (stonecrop): Another genus that offers plants in a wide variety of forms and colors, sedum is best for the sunny rock garden or as a modifying plant in any flower garden. There are varieties that support thirty-six to forty-inch succulent foliage; others grow as ground covers and are excellent border or small alpine plants.

VERONICA

Veronica (speedwell): Many species, most of which, but not all, have distinct flower clusters that occur along upright spikes. Colors range from purple and pink to magenta. A wonderful vertical accent in the sunny garden, nicest planted en masse and among other flowering plants, or as a border.

THE ECSTASY

The earth laughs in flowers.
—*Ralph Waldo Emerson*

Iris.

Black-eyed Susans (*Rudbeckia*)

Baby's breath (*Gysophylia*)

Coreopsis

Lobelia

Sunflowers (*Heliopsis)*

Summer phlox

Dicentia

Hosta

Iberis and phlox

Catmint *(Nepeta)*

110

GOOD GATHERINGS

Composition and Intersection

Composition: An arrangement of the parts of a work of art so as to form a unified, harmonious whole.
—Webster's New World Dictionary

Integration. Intersection. Association. Balance. Sound redundant? Well that's because I believe these are the keys to successful landscaping. Whatever elements you incorporate, you'll need to compose them, bring them together in some comprehensive way to be truly successful in the effort. Although any of the landscaping elements—walkways, flowers, shrubs, patios, et cetera, each stands alone in its beauty and purposefulness, it is their association with one another that creates a landscape. For instance, bringing a walkway sweeping through a garden can render both the garden and the walkway more beautiful. Introducing greenspace into a broad patio can create tremendous interest, softening the related hardscape elements and creating a great intersection.

We've talked about scale and placement of walkways and patios. We have to consider their association with all the other elements of the landscape. How do they blend? These aren't isolated things occurring on the property but rather part of a cohesive whole. Poor intersections can cause points or lines of tension.

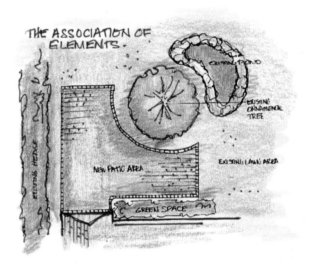

Intersections merit careful considerations and treatment. I think they can make or break a landscape. It's sort of like getting just the right rug to unite the furniture and decor of a room.

Intersections

Inside the home we seem very concerned about—and quite capable of handling—graceful and exciting intersections. The junction of floor and carpet, the width and length of curtains, the style of blinds, the levels and lines we create as we hang artwork, the way we display photos—these are all careful considerations we make inside the house quite easily. The seams of rooms—the halls or foyers where rooms meet—treated correctly can make all the difference. If we make a mistake, most of us notice the visual discomfort and change it. My experience tells me that we don't often do this outside. I've come to believe that similar intersections—the seams of the landscape, if you will—make all the difference. Look at these photos—the collision of varied landscape elements handled gracefully or dramatically.

Just as you do with your interior design (molding, trim, and so on), sweat the details outside.

Simple plant combinations

Many common plants have an uncommon presence when combined with others. Mixing plants means combining varied textures, subtle foliage colors, sizes, shapes—all plants differ and the difference, if used with some discretion, can make for a beautiful composition. Also, you need to make sure they all thrive in the same exposure: full sun, partial sun, shade, what have you. Plants can either bind or divide landscapes. Plants can frame, accentuate, or distract depending on their use.

Subtle foliage color and texture: Green laceleaf maple and hosta merge for interest.

Natural elements: Mountain laurel and birch intersect beautifully.

Texture is most important when combining plants. Putting together two or three plants with similar foliage and branch texture dilutes the character of each. If you have a glossy foliage plant, try combining it with a needled evergreen or a deciduous plant.

Form matters a great deal. Placing two similarly formed evergreens together takes away from each and creates visual discomfort. This is particularly true when using plants with a high degree of character or architectural form. They may compete, much like putting completely different furniture styles side by side in the living room or den.

Growth habit: Size matters. You'll need to know how large plants will get over time. As discussed earlier in "Caveat Emptor," growth habit is how the form of the plant will change over time. Size, mass, shape, and density can all change. Even color can alter with the age of a plant. (For instance, some plants lose vivid foliage or branch color with age and need to be cut back on occasion to encourage new growth.) The inherent difficulty here is that plants grow at a different pace, and sometimes the smaller plant at first will end up being the larger one in the end. In this case, knowledge is power. In cases like this you'll need to sacrifice immediate effect secure in the knowledge that the end will justify the means.

Color: Strangely, flower color may be the least important factor. Unlike perennials or annual flowers, most shrubs bloom for short periods. Chances are that only one of the plants in your combination will be in bloom at a time. To be safe, try combining flowering plants with nonflowering.

Density or visual depth: A plant that is dense and structural offers little visual depth. Although it may be attractive, a plant like this stops the eye rather than drawing it in. In many cases, such as screening for privacy or to frame a garden or lawn, this is desirable. We can direct attention with the heavy line of dense plants. We can narrow a frame of reference with heavy evergreens. We can frame a garden much like a picture is framed, with dense plants like buxus (boxwood) or compact ilex (hollies). On the other hand, plants with high visual character—colored or variegated foliage for instance—can be presented in the background of species that are loosely branched and lightly foliated. This creates visual depth, drawing the eye through one plant or group of plants toward the other. An example in nature is that beautiful clearing you come across in a forest where an opening in the tree canopy has allowed something of color to grow or flower. The distant beauty draws the eye to it while the thin woodland allows you to appreciate the depth and the varied layers of nature.

The "short list":

To get an idea of plant combinations, here are just a few that I have found to combine quite successfully, even dramatically. You can take this short list to a local nursery or garden center and see if they'd mind you moving a few plants into groups of three. Most won't. There's nothing better than an informed consumer. To help you think about form and texture, I offer simple silhouettes.

THINK OF PLANTS AS FORMS

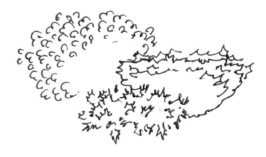

Azalea (rhododendron) /Juniperus squamata 'Blue Star' / *Picea nidiformis*

Ilex crenata / Potentilla / Thuja occidentalis 'Reingold'

Microbiota decussata / Rhododendron x. *myrtifolum / Viburnum* x. *burkwoodii*

114

Picea glauca 'Globosa' / *Weigela* 'Wine and roses'/ *euonymus* 'Gaiety'

Buxus 'Green Velvet' / *Chamaecyparis pisifera* "Gold Mop"/ *Spiraea*

Pinus cembra / *Kalmia minuet* / *Juniperus* 'Mother Lode'

Remember, when you first plant many of these shrub combinations, the size relationship can be off because plants grow at varied rates. This can make the process a little more challenging, so read the tag or research the individual plant a little. Seeing isn't always believing. Remember plants vary in their ability to withstand or thrive in particular climates. All plants are rated with a numerical system that relates to climate zones. When purchasing a plant, make sure it is rated for hardiness in your zone.

Combinations: See how the color, texture, and form vary, as well as the foliage and flower in this naturalized planting.

115

GOOD GATHERINGS

THE MASSES
ARE GRASSES

Ornamental grasses in the landscape

Tumbling together, the particles of air become a huge, unstoppable current. Some of them rake the earth, tousling grasses and trees . . . They have become the wind.
—*Jan DeBlieu,* Wind

Relatively new to the residential landscape in the eastern United States, few plants have been more celebrated and more misused than ornamental grasses. These beautiful stalks of grass that at their best mimic our prairies and ocean fronts can be a graceful and quite beautiful addition to the residential landscape. Their misuse usually parallels the parade of plants talked about in the chapter "Dressed For Success." Imposing our own understanding of plants as simple forms, we sometimes place tall grasses as a frame for smaller ones, often in a straight line, or we find a spot for an impulsively purchased plant that caught our attention at the garden center. Often we use an "informal plant" in a "formal" manner.

Better suited to massing as they occur in nature, ornamental grasses can look quite awkward in a garden filled with perennials or shrubs. They often seem an afterthought—and quite often they are just that, because when they're in their full glory in late summer and fall they're hard to resist. The proper way to use them seems to be en masse or in significant clumps of same species. Drifts or "waves" of the same plant can have a dramatic effect on the landscape. As a rear border they'll peek over other perennial gardens and offer significant privacy as a large mass. Obscured by a lower flower garden or other form, they'll dominate the landscape when the breeze lifts them and moves the plumes gracefully.

The forefront can be established with a shorter plant, layered just as we talked about layering other gardens. Or taller varieties can rise from a sea of other plants such as sedum. The real beauty of these grasses is the translucent plumes of many of them, the feathery flowers that allow the sun to pause on its journey, and the soft shifting of their foliage in the wind.

Used as an accent ornamental grasses can interrupt and soften our view, or, like other plants, affect our view and perspective. Because of the complexity of their foliage (the blades of grass), they have innate depth and compelling presence.

Most have a nice presence through the fall landscape. I recommend leaving them in winter until they're beaten up by too many snowstorms or layers of ice. At that point, on one of those sunny winter days you can go out and cut them back to ground level. This may not be an easy task—many are vigorous in growth and may have thick stalks. (I've been known to cut them down with a chain saw.) But they're well worth the effort. You want to cut them back before new spring growth so you can keep the old growth out of the new.

Try the following to begin with. You can add or subtract from the numbers, but the layout should re-main as a woven, interconnected massing. Simply weave masses of varied grasses into and through one another. This can create great depth or the illusion of depth as well as aesthetic interest. Find an area of the yard where you can experiment a little and enjoy these unique plantings.

Maiden grass (*Miscanthus sinensis 'Gracilimis'*) forms a large mass of foliage sporting a feathery silver plume in late summer that will remain on the plant into fall. Feather reed grass (*Calamagrostis* x *acutiflora* 'Karl Foerster') is a distinct and sturdy clump that can reach five feet in height. Blue fescue (*Festuca glauca*) and Blue oat grass (*Helictotrichon sempervirens*) form compact mounds of silver grass, a perfect foil for dark evergreens or herbaceous perennials or a wonderful border to that garden path you're constructing.

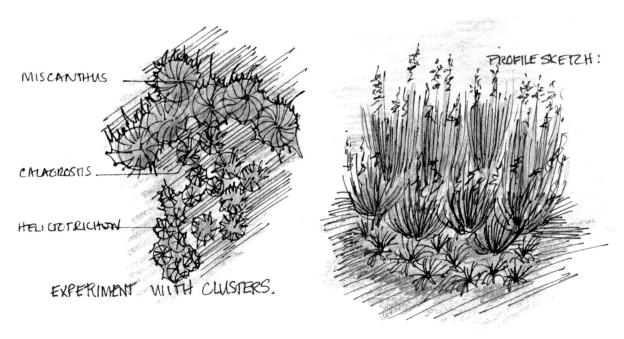

MISCANTHUS

CALAGROSTIS

HELICOTRICHON

EXPERIMENT WITH CLUSTERS.

PROFILE SKETCH:

Blue fescue (*festuca glauca*)

The Short List

Here's a short list of some of my favorites, all of which are quite hardy and easy to use.

Calamagrostis sinensis (feather reed grass).

*Carex berggrenii (*sedge). Short metallic foliage.

Festuca glauca (blue fescue). 'Superba', '*ovina glauca* 'Elijah Blue', or 'Sea Urchin'.

*Helictotrichon sempervirens (*blue oat grass). Thick silver blades.

Imperata koenigii 'Red Baron' (Japanese blood grass). Burgundy and green foliage.

Miscanthus sinensis (silver grass). 'Autumn Light', 'Morning Light', 'Sarabande', *variegatus, zebrinus.*

Pennisetum alopocuroides: Fountain Grass: 'Hamelyn', 'Little Bunny', 'Little Richie', *orientale* 'Karley Rose'.

So as you use this new element in your landscape, do so with some restraint. If you're landscaping a beach house or you're ready to begin giving up your lawn, masses of grasses might be the answer.

Here are before and after photos of a house on Martha's Vineyard that I designed in the early nineties. There is no lawn, simply grasses, perennials, and stone paths.

Before

 After

Towering miscanthus serves as a screen as well as a foil for some art-work and a white astilbe. It has a dominant presence and needs some room, a great background to other plantings.

Some of the smaller grasses can be nice rock garden plants.

THE MASSES ARE GRASSES

Fescue and imperata highlight this garden.

Dwarf fountain grass *(Pennisetum)*

Feather Reed Grass (*Calamagrosti*s) and Fountain Grass

Use grasses to soften the hard-scape or lighten the visual weight of an evergreen bed or perennial garden. They can be beautiful accents with their innate simplicity.

Mimicking the wind.

Miscanthus sinensis "zebrinus" captures
the light in this garden

Softening hardscape

THE LIGHT DIVIDED

Stone walls, lyric and legacy

Something there is that doesn't love a wall,
That sends the frozen ground-swell under it,
And spills the upper boulders in the sun.
—Robert Frost

Three of the primary elements of design—form (or mass), line, and texture—are rarely more prominent than in the presence of stone, particularly stone walls. In New England stone walls provide a link to our heritage and history, almost like a spine connecting the past to the present. And because of this, particularly in New England, they belong in almost any landscape where space allows.

As wonderfully as the words of the poet Robert Frost resonate, if the "frozen ground swells under it . . . spilling the upper boulders," there's something terribly wrong with the wall. This is a perfect example of the separation of art and craft. Our old farm walls, those often found now running through overgrown forest and field, are walls built of necessity for the most part. Farmers clearing the rocky ground to plant have, for centuries, dragged the stone to the borders of their land and piled the stone into walls. Some of these walls had purpose—to keep livestock in or out, to mark the property line. And although they reflect the inherent strength and integrity of stone, they are often built with minimal thought to engineering. These are the walls from which "boulders spill." And this is part of their beauty and charm: that single tumbled stone forming of an arc of overgrown grass. There's truly a lesson in this, an accidental bringing together of elements. ("All art imitates nature.")

These are stone walls at their best. They are some of New England's true historical and cultural monuments, reflecting the tireless labor of our ancestors. Stone dug from the ground with poor tools, was used for foundations of homes and barns, fences, paths. You can literally follow these walls as a path into our past. Quite often now overgrown with forest, imagine the field and you'll have a glimpse into history.

Never more obvious is the perfection of imperfection. Like the exaggerated lines or brushstrokes of the impressionist and abstract painters, the innate beauty of the stone wall is in the seams and spaces: the lichen colored skin mixing blues and greens and colors in between, the red of bleeding iron deposits, and the glistening silver of garnets and mica. Combining a sense of design, an understanding of physics and engineering—the result can be magnificent, a wall that soaks up the sun's rays as if they were returning to some source. It's the understanding of this exchange that elevates the construction as well as the presence of the wall. Though granite gray, in the low light of morning and evening the colors and shapes of a field-stone wall can be simply dazzling, bold slashes of shadow and light—the mass of itself heavy with precise shadow along the ground.

So if there's room, find a place for a stone wall in your landscape or garden. It will create a timelessness that is otherwise difficult to achieve.

Old stone, long exposed to the air, might be covered in lichen or moss, sanded smooth by the wind and rain. If you don't have the advantage of some of

this true "field" stone and you have to dig up shards of rock from the ground, this will age eventually as well. Time and weather, nature as the true artist.

We use stone on the landscape for varied purposes, and it is always a bold element. Used as borders, walls, retainers of soil and grade, sitting walls, framing elements, or simply ornamental accents or background—stone walls take a grand swipe out of the air and fill it with strength and a sense of place and time. There is even a sense of weight and strength. Look how they bind the terraces in this photo.

Perfect imperfection

Negative space

Just as in the garden—and all conceptual art—negative space is a vital element in the construction and appreciation of a stone wall. In fact it's what you see most: The space between the random shapes of the stone provides the real character of the wall. That most important of rules, "One on two, two on one," in fact speaks to the separation, the defining edges of the material. In the dead of winter, this serpentine dividing line is truly celebrated as windswept snow rests in the shadowed crevices while the sun clears the surface of the heated rock. It is that art, inherent in nature and explored and exploited.

Thick line drawing of the serpentine line of a stone wall.

Stone walls make wonderful borders, here separating lawn and garden. It's a comfortable evironment.

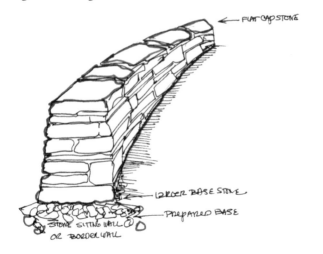

The quarry. Photo by Randy Anagnostis.

The Nature of Stone

Fieldstone is just what the name implies: found in our pastures and fields along old farm borders, dug from the ground just as farmers and ranchers have done for centuries. To my eye this is the most beautiful stone, and the true craftsman's touch is required to build a sound and beautiful wall of it.

Quarried stone is stone actively mined and quarried from the surrounding hills and mountains, usually with the use of explosives; then it is cut or snapped with machinery. Its geometric shape makes it actually easier to construct a wall with than the irregular and round form of fieldstone. From an engineering standpoint it can be more structurally sound.

A wall of stone from the quarry.

Formed concrete: Though hardly a comparison to natural stone, there are many prefabricated concrete block systems that are extremely functional and often attractive. The advantages might be the lower cost and the pre-engineered nature of the product, which allows a wider range of craftsmen or -women to install them effectively. Without endorsing a particular product, here is an example of a wall built from prefabricated concrete block.

Brownstone is also mined from quarries. It's soft stone, brown in color.

A bold stroke

Used as the bones or anchor of a garden, as the boundary of a property or a space, or simply as a beautiful and bold feature, stone walls in any form are a great addition to any landscape. In many ways they can serve as a broad trim to frame the space of the landscape. Besides their obvious utility, they can be an accent piece or a unifying element.

131

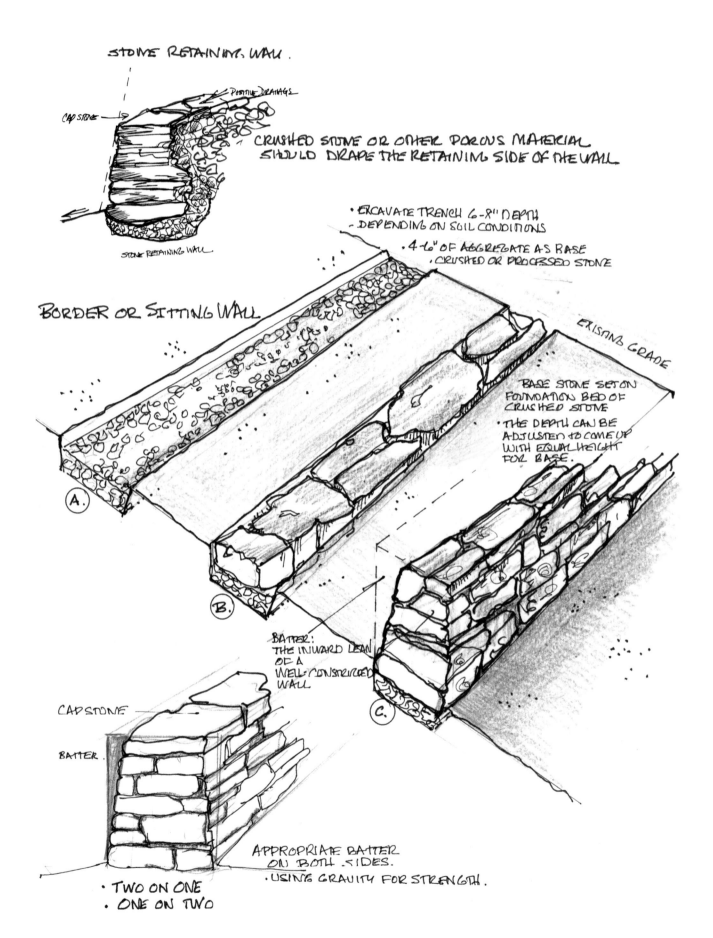

STONE RETAINING WALL.

POSITIVE DRAINAGE

CAP STONE

CRUSHED STONE OR OTHER POROUS MATERIAL
SHOULD DRAPE THE RETAINING SIDE OF THE WALL

STONE RETAINING WALL.

- EXCAVATE TRENCH 6-8" DEPTH
- DEPENDING ON SOIL CONDITIONS

- 4-6" OF AGGREGATE AS BASE
- CRUSHED OR PROCESSED STONE

BORDER OR SITTING WALL

EXISTING GRADE

- BASE STONE SET ON FOUNDATION BED OF CRUSHED STONE
- THE DEPTH CAN BE ADJUSTED TO COME UP WITH EQUAL HEIGHT FOR BASE.

A.

B.

C.

BATTER:
THE INWARD LEAN OF A WELL-CONSTRUCTED WALL

CAPSTONE

BATTER.

APPROPRIATE BATTER ON BOTH SIDES.
- USING GRAVITY FOR STRENGTH.

- TWO ON ONE
- ONE ON TWO

132

Retaining walls: These are stone walls that retain two different elevations. This is covered in detail in other chapters. Any of the stone types can be used to create retaining walls, but careful attention has to be paid to pitch, drainage, and backfill.

Multiple grades create both challenges and great opportunities. Some of our most beautiful landscapes are created along elevated or sloping ground. If the slopes are too difficult to garden or maintain, you might want to create level terraces or outdoor "floors." Think of it as a split-level house. Stone or other materials like wooden timbers ("timber cribs") can be used to retain the upper grade and segregate the levels.

Special attention must be paid to the ability of the construction to retain the grade. Some of this will relate to the composition of the soil. Soil that is very sandy or has a high gravel content might be easier to re-

tain, allowing a more free movement of water through it and behind the retaining wall. Soil that is thick with clay will have to be drained more carefully. The movement of water is the key here. The pressure of water and the freezing of moist ground could cause heaving and bulging in any wall not well considered or constructed. This is what "spills the upper boulders in the sun."

Stone steps: The same applies to steps as to walls. All the same materials are available and can be used with great artistry in creating steps. Either free-standing through gardens and sloping ground, or specifically connecting terraces, outdoor steps can be a real focal point in the landscape.

Besides providing access, they can be a great place to display potted plants or art objects.

Sitting walls: Like most border walls, these are two-sided walls. They can be used to frame an open space or patio. Generally constructed to eighteen- to twenty-inch height, just like an indoor chair, these can be great landscape features.

133

THE CRAFT

Dry stone wall construction

Preparation: Excavation is directly related to site and soil conditions. Once again, if the soil is heavy with clay and retains more moisture, the trench in which you'll establish the foundation of your stone wall will need to be deeper. If soil composition is sandy or rocky, the depth may not need to be much at all. A general rule would be from six to ten inches deep.

Drainage issues affect this as well. If you're constructing a wall at a high relative grade where water sheds away naturally, the base may be less critical. If your wall is to be constructed at a low point where moisture collects or stands, you'll need to pay more attention to base and backfill, finding a means to move water away from the construction. This can require drainage piping.

Natural stone: Using natural stone to construct walls, either fieldstone or stone excavated from quarries, is an inexact science. It takes a great deal of patience and some experience(and I think I've made a case for the creative eye) to create a beautiful and structurally sound wall from natural material.

After you've excavated a trench, six to eight inches wider than the anticipated width of the wall, fill the base with some form of aggregate. This can be larger crushed stone or processed gravel and is once again determined by the particular site. Larger aggregate (one to two inches) allows for easier movement of moisture though it. Crushed stone is angular and therefore knits better than washed or rounded stone.

Two on one, one on two: This principle of alternating the seams is a key to both the aesthetics and structural integrity of the wall. The basic elements of construction are weight and gravity. Essentially, the wall should lean into itself so that it uses gravity. This is called the batter. A general rule is two inches for every one foot of height, but on lower walls this is not necessary. Some masons construct batter boards which are cut to the "lean" of the surface of the wall so they can use them as a template to build without calculating. Freestanding walls will be constructed with outside walls that lean inward toward the core. Two-sided walls (sitting walls or traditional border walls) may have a core of smaller stone or gravel that will not be visible. Retaining walls or single-sided walls will lean into the grade they retain and be backfilled with gravel or crushed

stone to provide for the free movement of water.

Base stones should be larger and have shapes that will settle well into the flat surface of the prepared base. They should also offer a decent foundation surface from which to build.

Anchor or bonding stones are larger stones that will permeate through from side to side or from the front surface right into gravel of the retained grade. They are used to lock smaller stones into place and help secure the structure.

The placement of individual stones into the wall is where the true art begins to occur. Patient selection and placement are the keys to a solid construction and achieving a beautiful surface (often called the "skin" of the wall). Alternate seams and sizes, also laying the stones flat as they would naturally fall whenever possible. Continuous seams through layers of a wall will create structural weak points. Imagine the stone falling away at the seams.

Fitting and shimming: Fitting flatter stones in and around round or curved-faced ones is part of the art and joy of this process. Experienced masons read the natural seams of stone formed during the sedimentary process of their formation and use hammer and chisel to open seams and expose new flat surfaces of stone for construction. Masons may also use pieces of stone broken off or shattered from larger stone to shim and secure some of the junctions as well as for infill at the core of a sitting wall or behind a retaining wall.

Quarried, flat stone is generally easier to use because it offers multiple flat sides. The same construction techniques apply.

Capstones are generally large flat stones that finish off the top surface of the wall with some consistency. Although I wouldn't try this at home, I've heard you're supposed to be able to ride a bike across the surface of a perfectly executed atone wall. Like much of this work, the selection and size of finishing capstones is a very subjective process.

Manufactured stone (prefabricated wall block) is a different system altogether, but the same preparation and excavation are suggested. These walls come with their own specific construction recommendations and are pre-engineered (they have a built-in batter, for instance) so that some of the mystery is removed from the process.

This is ancient work and should be approached with the appropriate degree of respect for the craft.

THE LIGHT DIVIDED

Riches, riches, everywhere, just for the paying of attention. Even in two stones on one, one stone on two.
    —John Jerome

LAWNS MORE OR LESS

The usefulness, beauty, and headaches
inherent in growing grass

*Grass grows under my feet in front and back and
flowers come into bloom when they are supposed to.*
—*Joseph Heller,* Something Happened

Lawns garner a lion's share of attention in the residential landscape. For many of us, the quality of the lawn grass is the litmus test of a successful landscape. We spend an inordinate amount of time, energy, and money keeping it mowed and weed-free and that particular shade of green that we use as a measure of success. We share, with neighbors and friends, stories of our successes and failures in battling the varied diseases and invasive weeds that want to encroach on this delicately balanced ecosystem. I believe "lawn envy" is a significant element of the suburban domestic social fabric. (I admit to having experienced this myself.) An enormous industry is built on the maintenance and

health of lawn grasses. It's a significant part of our warm growing season for better or worse.

Like most of our gardening traditions, the residential lawn comes to us from England. The climate of the "mother country" was, however, far more suitable to grass lawns, and the acreage much less. The multibillion-dollar lawn industry in this country has helped to create unrealistic models for the perfect lawn. In fact, a slightly brown lawn in summer is the plant's natural reaction to the warm temperatures, a period of dormancy not unlike that brought on by the frigid winter months. The brown lawn is unacceptable these days as lawn care becomes ingrained in our innate competitive spirit and our quest for that perfect green carpet.

Yes, yes, yes. It's your province—your piece of the world. Isn't it? You've sown it and fed it and tamed it with the pure power of that shining machine in the garage. Even if the lawn area is small, it provides that palm of familiar green, that most simple oasis in a distracting world. And I won't wish that away from any of us.

It gives us among other things, visual relief from the complex color, form, and texture of gardens and hardscape. It can become part of the garden design, offering that clean forefront space beyond which flowers are presented. And it's in this visual simplicity where both its value and its inherent problems lie. If the lawn space is interrupted with encroaching weeds or empty space where insects have devoured the grass plants, or if the color is inconsistent—the green space is robbed of its visual simplicity and works less effectively in the design of a landscape. So we do have to cultivate the lawn space appropriately. But by the limiting the space, this might be less of a concern and our efforts more effective.

Lawns, certainly in spring and summer, provide a certain pool of light, that pause in the landscape that allows or perhaps invites consideration. It provides a canvas where the sun can paint its journey through the day. Actually hundreds of thousands of individual plants, lawns may be at their best when they draw little attention to themselves—but rather bring out the best in all things they are associated with.

Although the science and pathology of growing healthy lawns is a huge discipline, from a design standpoint lawn spaces are shape and color and perfect simplicity. A sweet curve of poor lawn might be more pleasant to view than a green square carpet of perfect lawn. And although we may admire our neighbor's perfect lawn and the countless hours he or she might put into its maintenance, the image we're more likely to remember is the sweep of a meadow or a mowed field in nature—even the gentle curve of the golf fairway. It's about shape and compelling line. It's about intersections. It's about pleasing line and dynamic shape. It's about design.

Lawns have a long history, having served as a surface for games since medieval times. And this may yet be their primary endearing purpose, a good game of Wiffle ball or volleyball, maybe a little croquet as in, perhaps, a more civilized day. But the areas used for this should be identified, graded appropriately, a good healthy rye-and-bluegrass mixture of seed used to support the summer games. This is all wonderful stuff. But consider this, when it comes to lawns: Less is more.

In no situation is this more true than in considering lawn areas. For the broad expanses of lawn many of us are used to, the days are numbered. Limited resources and heavy feeding requirements render the unlimited sprawl of grass of past generations obsolete. Constant irrigation will eventually test even the moist climates. The word *xerigraphic* has entered the landscaping lexicon, referring to plants and plantings that are drought-tolerant (and therefore good partners on the planet). Furthermore, lawns really look their best when reduced and framed with gardens or other elements of the landscape.

Lawns are an important design element. In truth, our lawns mimic nature's meadows, or at least they should. Have you ever had the opportunity to hike a thick forest, succumbing to the cool shade and then seeing the shafts of light that lead you to a beautiful open meadow? Here's the grass at knee height bending in the breeze and the sun uninterrupted engulfing you. It's a wonderful relief: one of nature's true art forms. But consider if it were all meadow, without contrast. Consider the plains of the Midwest, beautiful in their own right but even moreso in relief. We are blessed in the States with abundant variety. And in a way, our residential landscapes can do no better than mimic this grand scheme. Some of the most beautiful stretches of grass we see are the greens and fairways of the world's golf courses—almost always framed with "roughs," serpentine lines cut across them to make them appear as if painted across the ground. There is no reason we can't achieve the same effect in our home landscape. Define the purpose and the need and limit your lawn to those requirements. You'll be excited by the creative tension of its limits, in contrast with the boring story of endless expanse. It will take half the time to mow. And planned properly (although you may love using the old weed wacker), it should require no trimming.

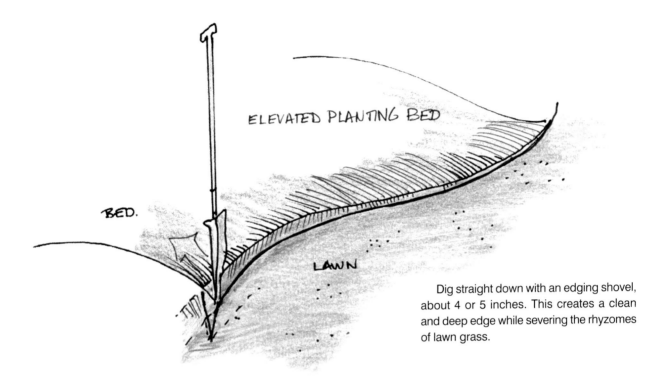

ELEVATED PLANTING BED

BED.

LAWN

Dig straight down with an edging shovel, about 4 or 5 inches. This creates a clean and deep edge while severing the rhyzomes of lawn grass.

Edges are everything.

No matter what size the plane of your open lawn, cut precise edges to it in soft curves.

This provides something easy and pleasant to look at. And in doing this we introduce another exciting design element: shape or line. Now besides color and form we have a distinct and pleasing line to mix with and complement all the others in the landscape. The sweet curve that distinguishes the back forty can be an art form in and of itself.

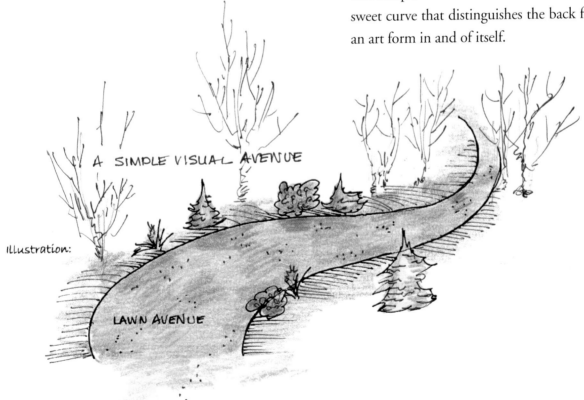

A SIMPLE VISUAL AVENUE

Illustration:

LAWN AVENUE

Forgive me but I think the lawn is a "man thing," and I don't want to be a traitor to the cause. It's a little like barbecuing. We can never let you women know how easy it is really, and how much we enjoy it. If we did, we wouldn't get as much credit for it, would we? Well, mowing the lawn can offer that same escape and release for many of us. That slight scent of oil and gas, mixed with fresh cut grass—it's almost like a steak sizzling on the grill. And with the sound, we can't hear a thing. We're not ignoring you. We're just busy cutting grass. And we know if you're doing the mowing, the same applies.

Along with all the elements of the landscape, the lawn has a separate and distinct character. In the case of grass, form and color are its most important elements. We want it simply to be perfectly flat and perfectly green. Even it rolls over hill and dale, we need the blades cut precisely at a consistent height. And because of this, we definitely overfertilize and overmow in most cases. I understand the uneasiness when the grass looks a tad too high and even more so when it looks uneven. It looks so darn good when fresh cut,

doesn't it? But the truth is, we should never mow more than a third of the height of the grass at one time. Less is more here as well. Let the blades stay nourished and root more deeply in the soil. Let the cut grass fall where it may and decay to nutrients in the soil. A "mulching mower" is best here, one that pulverizes the grass clippings into a nutrient stew. This will create and sustain a good organic soil and allow for deep root systems and strong rhizomes. The deeper the roots, the healthier and more disease-resistant will be the lawn. These mulched-up grass clippings are the best provider of nutrients to the lawn.

Weeds: "The best defense is a good offense"

That's right. A healthy, deeply rooted lawn will fight hard to preserve itself. A babied lawn, fertilized and watered constantly, will generally be more susceptible to the many diseases that want to settle into your back forty. Too much fertilization with nitrogen causes a buildup of thatch, which can suffocate the crown and root of the grass. Nitrogen can initiate vigorous leaf or blade growth without an appropriate root system: all foliage and no focus.

But here's another problem that we can include in the "nothing's simple" category. The truth is that on any given property, there might be varied zones, just as there are for other plants. Exposure and orientation vary on all sides of your house. Shade trees impact the surface, as do tall fences and walkways; and all affect the associated lawn. Part of your lawn might be in a blistering full day of sunshine, while another patch cowers in the quiet shade. These areas need to be cultivated differently, watered differently, and treated very differently. While bluegrass and rye can tolerate and thrive in the full sun, the areas in the shade will need to have a mixture of seed that contains some fine fescue. The shade grasses are weaker in stamina and stature, not much for games. Here's a place to accent the soft green plane with daylilies and daffodils. No football games here. In these shady spots the land is a mere ornament and an important cover for erosion control. The beauty will be in its pale green and the way the shadows drape themselves across it, soft and long in the morning and evening, precise in the full embrace of the summer sun. There's so much more going on here. Don't be so busy fertilizing and mowing that you miss it.

"You're in deep shade mister"

Forgive me a paraphrase? I'm not sure who might have said that, or if it's simply a saying misconstrued, but it's a perfect segue into the areas of your yard that will support lawn, and those that will need alternatives.

Although there are specific grass seeds to cultivate in shade such as fescue, dense shade may be an area to consider alternatives. There are perennial flowers that thrive in the shade: hostas, astilbes, lamium, and more. When I was growing up on Long Island my father's lawn turned to moss as the trees' canopy spread above it. Though my mother occasionally complained, I remember the soft beauty of the space as well as the fact that I no longer needed to mow it. Although no landscaper, my father's practice was prescient, as a few years after his death a feature article appeared in the *New York Times* regarding the beauty and simplicity of "moss lawns." Somewhere he was smiling, I'm sure.

Grass paths

Hidden avenues or paths of lawn bordered by gardens can be beautiful connecting arteries to areas or outdoor rooms. Simply keep them wide enough to mow easily. Reduce and open to broader spaces, much like hallways and foyers. Gardens or structures such as arbors can be wonderful elements to achieve this.

The real role of lawns

So my inclination is that in the case of lawns, less is more. Shape, appreciation of line and edge and

Framing with gardens or stone walls

inviting paths, both visual and practical through the landscape and gardens, should be the real role of lawns. By limiting the areas of lawn, we should be able to cultivate more easily and spend fewer hours and less energy sustaining and maintaining it. And by creating compelling edges and lines, we create a dynamic landscape with visual excitement. Think about the image you might have in your mind of the perfect lawn space. It might be the fairway of a golf course, the home of our most perfectly manicured lawns. But the image is a serpentine shape, isn't it? Framed in garden or roughs, it is a simple brush-stroke of green and not a boundless field of grass.

My contention is that the edges make it appear beautiful, not the expanse but the limits. It is color and shape and dynamic line, the forefront or the foil to other elements of the landscape. Broad paths (the expanse at least equal to your mower width) can invite the eye and create visual depth and interest, while gentle curves keep the mowing easy and the trimming to a minimum.

Of course there is also the very practical function of the lawn, and that is for recreation and open space. But I think in the domestic landscape these functions

143

There is no question that our nearly sacred lawn spaces are here to stay. They are much too entrenched in our expectations of the landscape to wither anything but very slowly. But if watering and fertilization continue to be problematic, then wither they will. I think our lawn space should be thought out and considered as a single element of the well-considered landscape. Lawns should be limited to our needs and used as the beautiful negative space on the canvas of our landscapes. At its best, an expanse of lawn provides a perfect pool of light on a summer morning, the shadows of bordering plants drawn gracefully across it. At its worse it can be a voracious consumer of water and fertilizer. In the case of lawns, like so many things we value in our lives: *Less is more.*

and requirements should be considered and created accordingly, as well thought out as the spaces inside the home.

Lawns where children play can be bordered with the bright colors of flowers and shrubs, or with plants of compelling fragrance or shape. While maintaining a large enough play area, a vegetative buffer can serve as a visual border and a reminder to children of certain limitations, an outdoor room. Areas for recreation such as volleyball or playing catch with a baseball require particular spaces: for a volleyball court you'll need about seventy feet by forty feet, and if you hope to bring up an outfielder you'll need even more to shag flyballs. But all of these spaces can be considered and included in a well-designed landscape. And the landscape can be planned to change as the needs of the family change. The gardens can grow while the lawn area shrinks as the children's needs change, or vice versa.

PLACE AND PRESENCE

Ornamental and shade trees
in the landscape

I frequently tramped eight or ten miles through the deepest snow to keep an appointment with a beech tree, or a yellow birch, or an old acquaintance among the pines. —Henry David Thoreau

The lasting memory of many natural landscapes, certainly to the casual observer, is often of the dominant trees: the great maples and oaks of New England, the cypress bending away from the sea along California's coast, the quaking aspen and the snow laden blue spruce of the Rockies, the swaying palms and bright magnolias of the South. Trees are the exclamation points of the landscape, the masters of their domain. They control light and perspective and scale. Many of us may be unconsciously drawn to landscaping by the experience of picnicking or reading under a grand tree in a park or yard: leaning against the warm, wide trunk, feeling the cool air, watching the dance of shadows beneath us as a breeze kicks up. Trees can be the anchors of a landscape. They should be chosen carefully, considering form and flower. They are an architectural element as well as a beautiful addition to the garden or yard. They are the ceiling of the landscape. Their roots are the basement. And their placement is always critical: determined by function and practicality. At their best they are a focus of a well planned landscape. They can be dominant and can become, at their worst, to paraphrase *Saturday Night Live,* the things that wouldn't leave.

There are so many encyclopedic books on trees, and so much information available from arborists, that I'll confine my attention to a brief discussion of the role of trees in the residential landscape. I think we can break them down into these categories: shade, ornamental, screening, and fruit bearing. The two most common features for which we use trees in the home landscape are shade and ornament. Shade trees generally have a wide and dense canopy, while ornamental trees have specific character or attractive flower or berry. A sugar maple (*Acer saccharum*) would be a typical large shade tree, while a dogwood (*Cornus florida*) would be considered an ornamental. The characteristics aren't exclusive, obviously.

An important consideration is the mature size of the tree. Caveat emptor, remember. What you can fit in your trunk next Saturday may be the most dominant feature in your entire neighborhood in ten years. Read the tags carefully and ask some questions. The web is a great place to check this information.

In the marketing of deciduous trees (those that lose their leaves in winter), sizes are specified in either height or caliper. For trees grown by a nursery for the marketplace, the size and value are determined by the caliper: the diameter of the trunk eight inches from the ground (or from the top of the rootball). Usually

145

when you're purchasing a tree of this size you'll have to consider a truck and perhaps a small backhoe for planting.

Basic Forms

As far as design goes, consider the form of the mature tree. Trees have some basic forms with obvious variety.

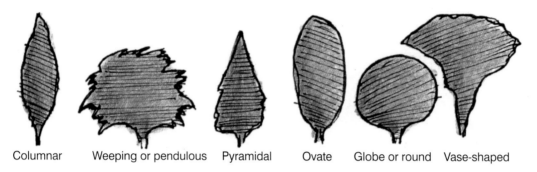

Columnar   Weeping or pendulous   Pyramidal   Ovate   Globe or round   Vase-shaped

What lies beneath?

The hole for the rootball of a tree should be dug to twice the diameter across the rootball and one and a half times the depth. But you're not planting at this depth. Take the best of the soil (rock-free and rich) you've excavated and put it back into the bottom of the whole. This removes the mystery of "what lies beneath." If you've excavated deep enough, you can be comfortable in the knowledge that you haven't just dropped your tree on shallow stone ledge, an ancient crypt, a 1963 Volkswagen Bug, or anything else that might be impenetrable to new feeder roots. These are those thread-like fibers that retrieve water and nutrients from the soil. If your tree has been properly root-pruned and harvested at a nursery, these roots should be ready to continue their function in the new environment.

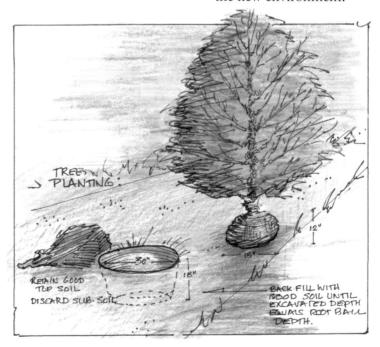

TREES PLANTING.

RETAIN GOOD TOP SOIL
DISCARD SUB-SOIL

30"

18"

12"

15"

BACK FILL WITH GOOD SOIL UNTIL EXCAVATED DEPTH EQUALS ROOT BALL DEPTH.

146

After you've gotten the depth right—and for most trees the depth of the hole should equal the depth of the rootball or mass—you're ready to drop the tree in. It's a good idea to put a few inches of water in the hole before you do this. Roll it or drop it in leafy-side up, I always remind my co-workers (at times with no signs of amusement on their part). With the good soil you've separated from the junk you've dug up, fill the void around the root system. Tamp the soil in so it's settled and won't sink anymore. It's a good idea to put some water in the bottom of the hole a few minutes before you backfill. If you haven't done this, then *water now.* A slow soak of the root system is the best way to treat the freshly planted tree or trees. You really need to water daily in the first few weeks after planting, and then a couple of times per week in that first season. Water the roots not the foliage. Your lawn irrigation system is not adequate to water the roots of a freshly planted tree. A small amount of mulch around the base of the tree should help keep the soil cool and moist.

Trees as part of the landscape

Trees can stand alone or be an anchor for a garden. Consider the amount of shade they will produce. This will affect your selection of underlying garden plants. Also consider root competition. Trees like maples that are supported by wide shallow roots can be difficult to plant under. If you want an associated garden rather than an isolated tree, you may want to extend it quite large and leave the area directly under the canopy mulched.

Most trees should have an area at their base free of lawn. This will keep you from having to mow or trim close to the trunk, which could damage the bark. Many diseases or insect problems begin at an area of bark damage. The bark protects the cadmium layer and the living tissue of the tree.

A good rule of thumb, aesthetically and practically, seems to be a third of the breadth of the canopy for a base bed. I think this is one of those rules that can be easily broken with few ramifications. Recall the art. When it comes to creativity, new rules are written every moment.

A RULE OF THUMB

The late afternoon sun bloomed in the window for a moment like the blue honey of the Mediterranean.
—*F. Scott Fitzgerald,* The Great Gatsby

If you have some cool Mediterranean breezes, this might be a great thing, but if it's mid-August in Somewhere, USA chances are that hot sun isn't that welcome. Shade the rooms from the hot afternoon sun, but allow morning sun into the house. Deciduous trees cool in the summer and let the light pour in during the winter months with a natural warming effect. They are one of nature's great provisions.

A general rule would be to plant evergreen trees on the north side for protection from colder air, and deciduous trees on the southern exposures for their tempering effect.

Inside out: What about from inside the house. When you are deciding the location of a tree of any kind consider the view from inside. An early-flowering tree like a magnolia or dogwood might look beautiful from the sunroom and can change the look and appreciation of the inside space. A properly located evergreen can corral your visual appreciation of the outside and bring your attention forward to smaller gardens. Are you trying to screen an objectionable view? Draw attention across an open span of lawn or gardens? A tree with brightly colored foliage (such as a Japanese maple or Newport plum) can be the focus of your view from certain windows or rooms. A weeping tree (weeping cherry or willow) can draw the eye back to some middle ground, perhaps a garden or living space such as a patio. You've probably done this inside your home with a certain lamp shade or chandelier. Consider the same outside.

The position of trees outside the home can affect the scale and perspective of the inside space. Try setting those stakes out and imagining the presence of small or larger tree. When planting trees of any kind, the most important considerations are place and presence.

Pink dogwood   White dogwood

Dogwood underplanted with hosta and other perennials.

Mimosa

Acer platenoides

148

THE CRAFT

Place and Presence: Installing Trees

You can dig it: Many trees, particularly larger ones, are dug and marketed as *B&B,* which means "ball and burlap." Once you've managed to get the tree to where you think you want it planted, mark the spot. With spray paint or any other means, mark a circle on the ground twice the circumference of the rootball. This will be the size of the hole you'll need to dig.

If there's lawn grass established, you'll need to strip this away first and expose the topsoil. In most cases the best soil will be in the top eight to ten inches from the surface. As you're digging, keep this better soil in a pile separate from rocks and sandy soil or gravel. Remember, you'll be displacing soil with the volume of the new rootball; you can use the better soil to fill back in around the new rootball and get rid of the rest.

Although the tree will be planted at the height of the rootball, you should dig a hole at least six inches deeper (check with a tape measure) than the depth of the ball. This way you'll be sure there are no unseen boulders or ledge that you're about to sit your beautiful new tree on. The new roots need some room to get started.

Note: The height of the rootball at finished grade should be slightly higher than the surrounding grade. This allows for inevitable settling of the new plant.

Once you've cleaned to the depth, restore good topsoil until you're at the right height.

Do not remove the burlap. Lift or roll the rootball in, being careful to protect the trunk and branches from damage. Once it's in, you should be able to straighten and adjust the tree. It's hard to lift out however, so double-check your measurements before you drop it in.

Some large trees with large rootballs are also bound with wire cages. In most cases these cages should be left on: Roots will find their way through. The worst thing for a large tree that has been root pruned and bound in a ball is for the ball to fall apart. You want to accomplish this transplant while disturbing the rootball as little as possible.

Container trees—those grown or marketed in pots—should be planted the same way. Disturb the roots as little as possible, even though soil is more apt to fall away from a container-grown tree.

Irrigate: It's not necessary, but it's always better to plant in cooler temperatures and overcast skies. In all cases, water should be available to soak the roots during and after planting. This should continue for a few weeks after planting, until the roots have had some time to dig in and find their own water. For at least the first month, these trees are dependent on you for water and nourishment. You can fertilize root systems with bonemeal or super phosphate; the amount varies greatly with the size of the tree and the concentration of the fertilizer in the particular product.

After watering, tamp or compact the new soil around the tree to rid it of air pockets. These can collect water and cause frost heaves or other problems. A light mulching around the tree—without burying the taper of the trunk—will help keep the moisture in.

In most cases, staking is not recommended. Let these roots feed out and secure the tree.

You're done. Good work. It's time to plan the location and variety of your next tree. Before you know it you'll be made in the shade.

UPS AND DOWNS

Grading and terracing

It is the common lot of mortals to sustain the ups and downs of fortune. —Aesop's Fables

So it is (my apologies to Aesop) with landscaping. Difficulties abound but there is no question that many of our most endearing landscapes occur on spaces that are not level at all. I spent a year in San Francisco, and one of the beauties of the city is that so much fills the eye in a simple panorama. The cityscape occurs on so many varied planes that there is inherent excitement in the most casual view. The same can be said of the residential landscape. Although the homeowner is presented with challenges, these landscapes are well worth the effort.

Basic grading

The initial grade of a new house is one of the most critical landscape considerations. Before I go too far with this, let me say that many of these considerations are outside of the realm of the landscape designer. Civil engineers and other professionals trained in the subtleties of soil content, filtration capacities,

and other matters are the first resort here. But landscape designers or a homeowners should be able to consider, understand, and even affect drainage as part of their overall treatment of a property. For the purposes of this discussion, I'll illuminate some grading concepts and treatments that will help both new homeowners and established homeowners understand simple drainage issues.

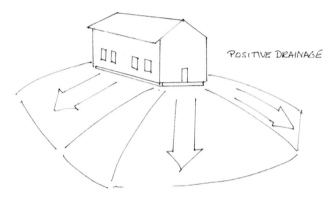

POSITIVE DRAINAGE

Foundation drainage systems

Proper grading is essential in the residential landscape. Obviously, you want to move water away from a foundation, whenever possible. Positive pitch, or a grade that allows surface water to flow away from the foundation is the most desirable. Even with positive pitch, most new homes have foundation drainage systems. These are pipes, usually PVC, that collect water along the outside of the house foundation and from the roof gutters and downspouts and move it toward an outlet. Perforations along the lateral pipe absorb groundwater and carry it away—keeping it from saturating the soil around the home.

TYPICAL FOUNDATION DRAIN

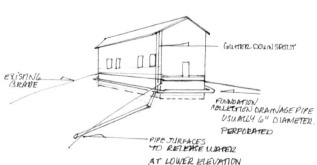

GUTTER DOWNSPOUT

EXISTING GRADE

FOUNDATION COLLECTION DRAINAGE PIPE USUALLY 6" DIAMETER. PERFORATED

PIPE SURFACES TO RELEASE WATER AT LOWER ELEVATION

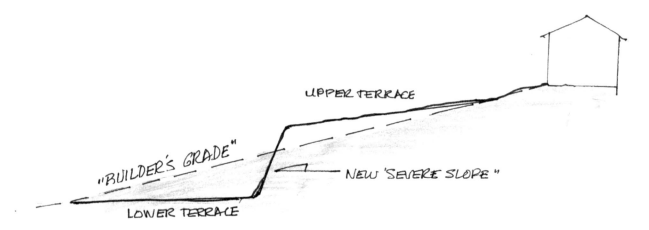

Though desirable, positive pitch can create its own problems. One of these is what I call a "builder's grade." In the best interest of the homeowner and a dry basement, and with the best intentions, many homebuilders simply create sloping grades away from the foundation to whatever lower associated grade exists. In some case this works fine. In others it creates a large area of lawn that is relatively useless because none of it is level, and presents an arduous task to mow. For families with a brood of kids, or simply someone who wants to create an enjoyable, interactive landscape, this may be quite impractical and undesirable. The solution in this case is terracing.

This creates two or more functional and visually compelling terraces, much like floors of a home (imagine particularly a split-level). These newly formed terraces can remain lawn or be transformed into wonderful gardens or patio areas—outdoor rooms open to the sky.

The new, more severe slope can be treated in a variety of manners. If it isn't too steep, a slope or rock garden can be established along it. There are many good ground covers (junipers, cotoneaster, microbiota, pachysandra, and more) whose shallow roots and dense foliage will help protect and bind the soil. Large boulders can be used to protect from erosion and act as the "bones" of a garden created around them along the slope.

The other solution would be the construction of a retaining wall to retain the upper surface and segregate the levels. While maximizing the usable area (the graduated slope takes up more room than does an immediate wall), retaining walls properly done can be magnificent additions to the landscape.

When retaining grade with a wall, whatever the particular material you choose, drainage remains an important concern. Retaining all of the moisture and groundwater of the upper terrace, these walls should have ample drainage material or treatment behind them. The strength and capacity to retain varies greatly with the makeup of the soil. For now we'll consider average soil. You'll need to judge your own when considering these options.

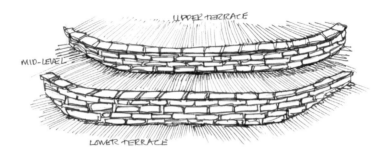

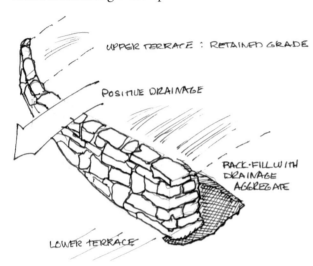

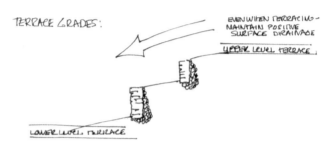

The mid-level terrace is a perfect spot for a garden: waist-high and easy to maintain.

If perennial gardens are planted on these terraces, they are visible from a completely different perspective. There are wonderful plants that will cascade over a retaining wall.

When establishing the upper terrace, be sure that the surface grade remains slightly higher than and pitched toward the wall. This allows surface water to shed over the wall. Having all of the water drawn and trapped behind a retaining wall is never a good solution. In cold areas like New England, this causes the heaving and blowouts of retaining walls.

Extreme grade changes may call for more than one wall or two terraces. A general rule in the residential landscape is to not exceed four feet with a single wall. If you need to retain more than four feet, you can divide the height with two walls. Generally the upper wall should be no bigger than, and preferably lower than, the lower wall. This works both aesthetically and structurally.

Appropriate drainage can be established with a combination of elements. Crushed stone can form a filtering void behind the wall and may be enough. Sometimes four- or six-inch flexible plastic pipe can be installed as well to keep the water moving behind the wall rather than settling in the soil. Depending on soil content and the kind of wall that's constructed, you may also need a pipe or several to allow an escape of moisture through the wall. Trapped water freezes. Freezing water and soil expand (or heave). The character of the indigenous soil is always a factor in these considerations. Soil varies greatly from region to region, sometimes even town to town. Many counties have soil composition studies available as it impacts all community development.

Retaining wall alternatives

There are more retaining wall alternatives than I can mention and probably more than I can even imagine. I've created some simple boulder masses to retain slopes, and I've seen many done beautifully. But the basics are below. Natural stone is always my first choice.

The planted slope.

Difficult grades literally have their ups and downs in the home landscape. Problems, however, can often become opportunities. You know the glass-half-empty-or-half-full routine. Well, think of the glass as half full of water. Terraces are perfect places to incorporate water features, particularly falls.

The nice thing about multiple terraces is that that they may call for steps, which—as we've already discussed—can be real features, true binding elements, in the garden: the grand staircase of your outdoor home.

Although they're quickly being replaced with pre-formed concrete block and other new wall systems, I have designed and constructed a lot of timber walls over the years. They remain a less expensive alternative.

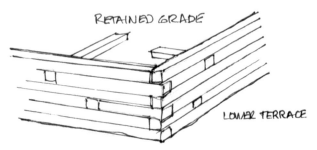

"TIMBER CRIB"

RETAINED GRADE

LOWER TERRACE

PERPINDICULAR SUPPORTS ARE CALLED "DEAD MEN" ANCHORS.

Be creative in your use of the middle terrace.

The key is to see the apparent disadvantage of sloping yards in a positive light, or as an advantage when it comes to landscape design. Your yard has built-in interest and character. It's sort of like that date with a "nice personality"—sometimes that can work out, too. Terraces can provide the most intriguing landscapes, visible from multiple viewpoints and providing multiple views.

TIMBER RETAINING WALL

The combination of large 8x8 timbers plus large washed stone, left exposed, creates an interesting retaining wall that solves a grade problem while celebrating the intriguing architecture of this contemporary home.

CRY ME A RIVER

Creative Drainage solutions:
Turning frustrations into focal points

"Your bridges got burned. Now it's your time to cry. Cry me a river." —Arthur Hamilton

Swales and berms are grade changes that you can make to alter the movement of water across the surface of the ground. Simply, a berm is an area of elevated soil or fill and soil. This can block surface water and redirect it while creating a raised bed.

A swale is a depression in the soil, usually a linear path of least resistance in which water can move across the land. If wide and gradual, it can remain as lawn.

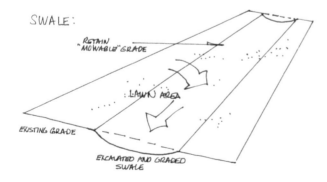

If it needs to be deeper and narrower, it can be filled with crushed stone. This is a simple drainage culvert usually called a French drain (I guess from the old open sewer systems in France) The culvert remains open and simply collects surface and groundwater and filters it away.

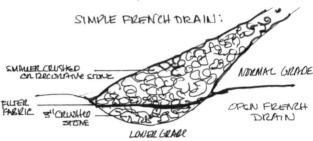

If the problem is acute and severe, and it's difficult to pitch the grade of a lawn or even a swale away, you may need to install underground drainage pipe. Simple collection boxes often called yard drains can be installed to collect the surface water and drain it though plastic or vinyl pipe underground. Obviously it will need an escape point or outlet, so the distance, difficulty, and expense can be significant.

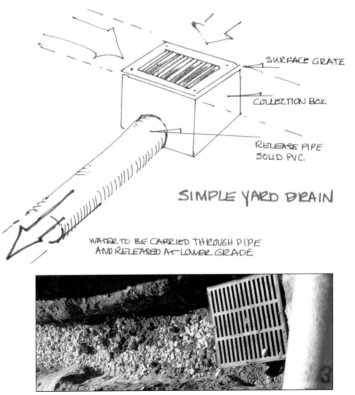

163

Cry me a river

Who needs open water? In fact you don't even need a drainage problem to consider the next idea.

The logical evolution of the open drain or swale is the "dry river bed" or "dry stream." Using the age-old creativity of the Japanese and their wonderful work with stone gardens, these swales can be fitted with all kinds of drainage systems and then be naturalized to look like river beds. Like any design, the selection and placement of material is critical. Choose natural stone, washed stone that looks weathered by water, or perhaps boulders that may look like they belong on the sides of a river and have been there for a while. Once again, although drainage may be a science, these mock river beds are an art.

This illusion of a river bed can disguise an elaborate buried pipe system, or simply be a benign way to move surface water across the property, an opportunity to have some fun with plants and stone.

MULTI- FACETED DRAINAGE SYSTEM

DRY RIVER BED

The path of least resistance: We designed, excavated, and built this "dry" river bed.
A huge rainstorm moved in before we were finished. It works.
Notice the stone bridge and the pillars that mark its location.

164

BRIDGING THE GAP

At the heart of landscape design is turning potential problems into wonderful features. You can use stone or wood to create a bridge over the drainage swale or trench. This might be become the perfect anchor for your next garden. And now that you've joined the ranks of landscape designers, you'll begin to see these minor drainage problems as opportunities.

A simple stone slab may form a bridge

NATURAL STONE BRIDGE
OVER 'DRY STREAM.

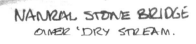

With wood, you can create any kind of feature you like.

ORNAMENTAL
WOODEN BRIDGE

BETWEEN A ROCK AND A HARD PLACE

Gardening with stone and unforgiving groundwater features

A fronte praeciptium a terg lupi.
(A precipice in front, wolves behind.) —Latin saying

Pulled from the ground—its absence providing an inviting pocket for soil amendments and plants—stone can be the perfect anchor for any garden. Since most of my work has been in New England, rock has evolved as an integral component of design. Maintaining a theme of turning problems into opportunities, stones can become a landscape element, even a feature. Although remaining something of an ancient mystery, it's clear that the stone slabs of Stonehenge were not brought in, but rather discovered and used to some mysterious purpose. There is that mystery inherent in gardening with stone. The contrast of the soft textures of plants with the rough lines of rock, the transformation of conflict (the stone, first discovered, is probably in the way) and effort toward inclusion and resolution. There's something perfect about this: that turning-problems-into-opportunities state of mind. There's something very symbiotic about a nice rock garden.

I've decided to include some water features in this chapter because in my mind they are really primarily about stone. Just like the riverbeds that appeared in the previous chapter, the design and creation of real water features in the landscape centers on the selection and placement of stone of varied shapes and sizes: once again, the association of elements. Placement and relationship to the landscape are important. Beside the selection of aquatic and surrounding plants, the rest of it is simply liners and plumbing—and of course fish.

Although in my work I've employed many of the lessons of the Japanese, I don't pretend to be an expert in Japanese gardens. There are so many dedicated practitioners and volumes of litereature on this particular art and craft (one that has developed over thirteen hundred years) that I'll simply give a nod of appreciation to those who are dedicated to this particular style of gardening and their inspiration. Serenity and harmony are keys to these gardens and are design elements that can be called on in all garden design.

The photos that follow show a small space garden where the art of Japanese gardening is employed. The carved stone, the washed pebbles, and the scale of the plants are borrowed from the concepts employed in Japanese gardens. Like all stone features, the garden takes on a beautiful and compelling winter presence as well. Traditional Japanese gardens use a lot of evergreens with architectural quality and a variety of stone for year-round beauty.

This garden area takes up less than twelve square feet, but is an important feature of a small yard.

This is a naturally hollowed stone. Simply by placing smaller washed stone in and around it, as well as some plants to soften, we've created an interesting garden focus, one that can change with the whims of the gardener by moving the smaller stones.

A key to any rock garden is the balance of plants to stone. Quite often we throw a few rocks into a garden and it looks just like that—like discarded stone rather than a rock garden. The size and placement of stone is critical, but once again is not a science. Use your designer's eye to come up with a balanced, harmonious combination of stone and plants. Remember thirds, and varying sizes, as discussed in earlier chapters. Proportion and texture are two important elements to employ in the creation of gardens that include stone features. Through the integration and placement of boulders, you're really breaking down the garden into smaller spaces, perhaps easier to imagine and manage.

Burying portions of the stone will help to make it look like it occurred in nature.

Rock Garden plants or Alpine plants

These make a nice complement to gathered rock or stone. They occur naturally in rocky or arid conditions. Here's a short list of plants you might considered for your rock garden. These are simply a few that I've used with some success. There are many more.

Shrubs

Cedrus atlantica 'glauca'; *c.a.* 'Pendula'

Chamaecyparis obtusa 'Coralliformis"

Cotoneaster

Hydrangea anomala subsp. *petiolaris*

Juniperus

Picea abies 'Pendula'

Pinus flexilis

Tsuga canadensis 'Cole's Prostrate'

Perennials

Achillea (yarrow)

Ajuga (carpet bugle)

Aquilegia (columbine)

Arabis (rock cress)

Artemisia (wormwood)

Campanula carpatica

Dianthus

Geranium (cranesbill)

Iberis (evergreen candytuft)

Lavandula augustifolia

Nepeta (catmint)

Perovskia (Russian sage)

Polemonium (Jacob's-ladder)

Salvia nemorosa (meadow sage)

Santolina incana (lavender cotton)

Sedum (stonecrop)

Sempervivum (hens and chicks)

Veronica (speedwell)

Yucca filementosa (Adam's needle)

Rocks as Sculptural Elements

Rocks can become part of the trend toward whimsy in the American landscape. Walking recently on an island in the middle of Lake Winnipesaukee in New Hampshire, I came across a residence, abandoned for the season, where the landscape was marked with several stone stacks. These were carefully and artfully created forms consisting of indigenous stone stacked into sculptural forms. Careful not to disturb them, I wished I had my camera with me. Coincidentally a month later I heard about a display of these stone creations at the New England Wild Flower Society's grounds in Framingham, Massachusetts. As man has since antiquity, these artists obviously see natural stone, with its inherent beauty, as an element of artistic expression.

One of the hidden beauties of the rock garden in New England is that the snow on the stone will melt before the surrounding earth or garden, creating a new expression of compelling shape and texture.

Water Features and Waterfalls

Water features are hugely popular in the landscape. Once again, I'll mention these as an element of design and leave the celebration of this particular craft to other books and other craftsmen.

From a design standpoint, the placement of natural stone can be the key to the successful creation of a garden pond or falls. The other important sensory ingredient here is the sound of the water over waterfalls. The height of the falls, the quantity or number of falls, the volume of moving water—all contribute to the sound. This element can be a wonderful way to muffle unwanted noise, the traffic of a nearby road, the voices of neighbors, and much more. All of these factors have contributed to the growing fascination with waterscapes.

Remember, landscape design is about layout and the association of elements. Water features can be a subtle or quite prominent feature of the landscape. Decide which you want yours to be. If it's located in a central part of the yard or near a deck or patio it will become a beautiful and dominant feature. If you tuck it away along the perimeter or behind a secondary garden, it can become a wonderful surprise and a distant intrigue. Ponds and waterfalls can become wonderful parts of an outdoor room. Or they can be situated close to an indoor space from which you can hear the calming sound of moving water. They are permanent features, much like a fireplace in the house. Is your primary fireplace in the den or the living room?

The location of the water feature and falls is a huge factor in smothering other sounds. One close by creates more immediate welcome sound than one placed on the perimeter.

Once again, the selection and placement of the surrounding and embedded stones are critical to natural design. The creation of the falls themselves often depends on either discovering good stones or purchasing them from a stone yard or quarry—or often a combination of the two.

The creation of the falls themselves is almost a separate art. Finding smooth, flat stones is key. Look for stones with a face that is flat or cuts in from the top. This aesthetic search is one of the joys of the process of creating water features.

If you can create a void behind a falls, you create a small "echo chamber" that can amplify the sound of falling water for a more dramatic effect.

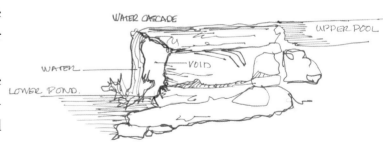

Larger rocks located at the rim can create stability for access to the water and the maintenance of a small pond.

The art and craft here is the knitting of smaller and larger stones to create stability while maintaining a natural look.

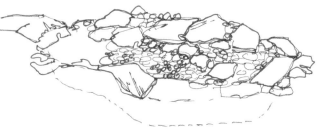

When the location, design, and installation of the water feature are complete, you're ready to consider the many aquatic plants and the fish that will create a healthy micro-environment. Since this book focuses on design, I'll leave these details to others.

The surrounding landscape is very important. You want there to be some sensible association. A pond plopped in the middle of an acre of lawn will probably never appear natural. The placement of a garden or small grove of trees can bind the water feature to the rest of the landscape. Think about scale and association. Remember: The eyes have it. Be a designer before you're a pond builder.

This pond connects an upper terrace to a lower patio, an integral part of an "outdoor room."

Excavate shelves on which to layer stone and aquatic, plants and for safe access and egress.

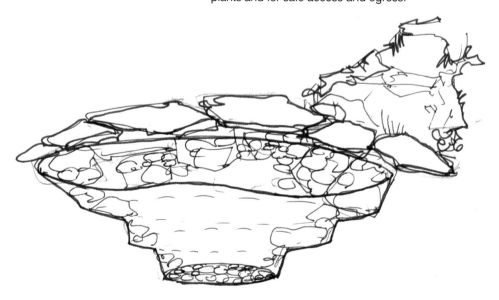

Stone blasted from the pool is used to form a massive rock garden slope.

"CEE-MENT" PONDS

Swimming pools and their place in the landscape

"Lookee Jed, it's a cee-ment pond."
—*Granny,* The Beverly Hillbillies

Ah, Granny Clampett was right, wasn't she? What most of us are really looking for is that perfect pond nestled into the backyard. Maybe it speaks to our rural Tom Sawyer heritage. Only this pond has crystal-clear water and often comes in a form far from natural. The oval, the rectangle, the kidney or whatever shape is used doesn't quite ring true in the *natural* department. With exceptions, most pools introduce a field of crystal blue on the greenscape of the yard: a focal point. So there are a number of different directions to take when considering the landscape layout that includes a pool.

A helicopter in the foyer:

No matter how active we might be as a swimmer, most of us spend a lot more time sitting near the water than we do in it. Pools are more often viewed than used, and in the average residential landscape that view may become the dominant one. This is why the consideration of the placement and the impact on the associated landscape is so important. Ill conceived, the pool can be a disaster. Imagine if after you've spent years decorating the interior of your home on a shopping spree, you decided to buy the helicopter prop from the Broadway play *Miss Saigon* and set it in your foyer or in the middle of the family room. The impact on the interior design would be similar to the arrival of the swimming pool as an element in the landscape. It can have, if not carefully considered, a white-elephant effect.

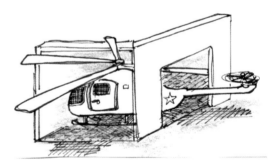

Given that I'm not an installer of pools, nor an expert on the mechanisms of the many types of pools available, I'll limit my comments to their presence and treatment in the landscape. I will say that I've designed around a lot of pools and found most in this industry very professional and usually sensitive to the micro-environment they're helping to create. And I've found others who are experts in swimming pool construction and mechanics, and fairly insensitive to the impacted landscape. Also, and I say this with a degree of respect and amusement, I've never heard a client told that his or her property wasn't suitable for a swimming pool. Where there exists a will, there is definitely a way.

Despite the limited seasons of the northern United States, swimming pools are becoming a more dramatic and considered landscape element nationwide. This is a good thing, as they're seen increasingly as an integral element even in the average suburban landscape.

A swimming hole. A hole filled with water. Ah, the perfect simplicity of the obvious. And in a very real sense, that's all swimming pools are, until you've worked to blend them with the surrounding landscape. Taking lessons from the beautiful pools of the southern and milder western climates, even New Englanders these days are considering pools for their effect as well as their function.

There are many types of pools, from aboveground circles to rectangles framed in decks. The in-ground pools that we'll talk about in this chapter range from vinyl liners to poured concrete or "gunnite" mixtures, creating more natural shapes. Although liners are becoming more varied in style and color, poured surfaces offer the chance to naturalize the color of the pool with dark paints that can mimic that "cement pond" look you might be seeking. I won't espouse the particular values of either one because price and purpose affect the decision. The basic principles of design apply to all. "The Landscaper Theory of Relativity" bears remembering.

Location

It seems to me the most important thing about the residential swimming pool is its placement—the association of the shape and presence of the pool with the surrounding elements. Obviously, full or mostly full sun exposure is important. Besides the obvious warming effect, the absence of deciduous trees in the

immediate location for the pool will help keep vegetative debris out of the water.

There is no correct or incorrect location for a pool, but you might consider the thirds of the artist's eye once again. If you're looking at your backyard, try to split it into thirds no matter what the actual size. The immediate third is your primary living and transition space. Usually this is occupied by a deck or patio, transition walks, and so on. The middle ground can be open lawn or gardens, and the back third might contain some defining border. Any of these three spaces is worth considering, but make the decision with a designer's eye. The most obvious spot for the pool might seem like the center of the yard. But put this on paper and you might see this central location as a "static" composition with everything revolving around the pool. Everything else will become secondary. As when deciding on a patio or outdoor room, your best bet might be to set up a site conditions drawing of your yard, then cut out a pool shape, correctly scaled, from a piece of colored paper and move it around the scale drawing until it seems to look right in relation to the other shapes and forms that fill the landscape. This will include the house (obviously), any outbuildings, major trees, and natural features. How does it relate? Remember to consider grade. Whatever your property's grade, the crystal-clear water of the new swimming pool will be perfectly level, as will the coping, or else of course it will be a perpetual falls . . . and that's a whole different discussion. If you don't have a level yard, a retaining wall (See "Ups and Downs") may be necessary. These can be some of the hidden costs of pool installation.

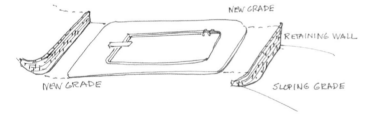

In this imagining stage, remember many pool companies have life-size templates of pool shapes they can lay out on the ground for you so you can see the impact of this important new presence. Your imag-

ined and intended use of the pool is an important consideration, as is the age of your children if you have a family. In the case of a family of young children, unobstructed view is a primary requirement. This, both for the pleasure of watching the kids having great fun and for the obvious safety concerns. Consider trying to integrate the pool into this first third of the yard where it becomes nearly an extension of the interior space.

If you hope to retain the integrity of your existing yard and landscape, you may want to consider creating the pool environment as a separate space on the property, in either the middle or the far third of the yard. Such pools can be hidden with fences and planting and be a pleasant surprise, an escape in the landscape rather than a primary focus—sort of like moving the helicopter into the screened porch.

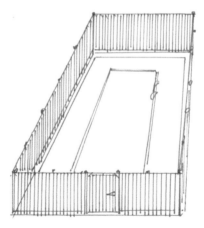

Fences

Unfortunately, it's impossible to consider a swimming pool without the required surrounding fence. All your illustrious design concepts can be rendered obsolete by the overpowering presence of the fence. All localities require an impenetrable barrier at least four feet high around the in-ground swimming pool.

This can either be a direct enclosure of the swimming pool, the enclosure of the entire yard, or some combination of both. But like the pickets of the deck railing that we discussed in earlier chapters, the fence becomes a primary design consideration. Just as it is with other design considerations, *the line of the fence is as important as, or sometimes more so, the particular type.*

Surrounding patios

Again, we spend a lot more time admiring the shimmering water than we do submerged in it. Make sure to leave enough space, and make it interesting. You'll need the obvious space for chaise lounges and tables. A simple suggestion is similar to one I've made earlier in this book: Rather than a narrow hallway (four feet of paving material around the entire coping), manipulate the bordering paving material to create some intriguing outdoor rooms. Don't settle on one; consider creating a primary entertaining area and a secondary one. (*Remember that those little kids, your children or grandchildren, will be teenagers someday, and you'll want to give them some space. Really.*)

Sometimes having a smaller patio across the pool, away from the house, allows a nice view back across the water toward the house. This is a simple but worthwhile design consideration—a secondary outdoor room. Don't hesitate to interrupt the patio areas with "pocket gardens," which are also great places to incorporate small and large rocks that may have been dug up during installation. Not too much, just enough.

Bring on the other elements

Now it's time for plants, stone, and more. The pool isn't an aberration in the yard but rather an integral part of the total cohesive scheme of your landscape. Integrate it with the landscape. There are obviously lots of types of swimming pools, and they're evolving all the time. There's a movement in Europe and other places to use natural ecosystems to control the quality of the water. This can mean actually having a shallow end filled with plants and associated wildlife, much closer to Granny's "cement pond." For the purposes of this book, however, these pools reflect the traditional liner or other in-ground pools.

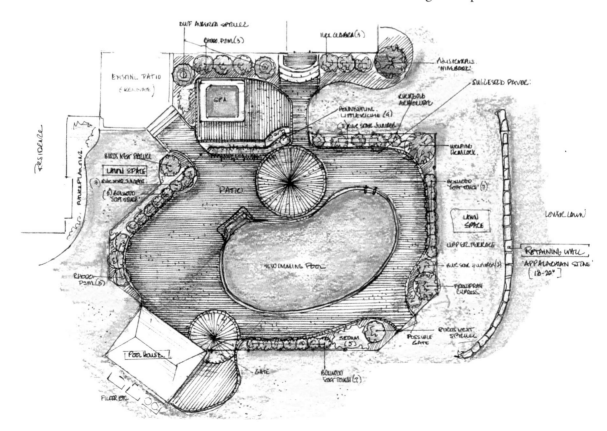

Here a waterfall cascading over a stone wall helps connect the terraces, uniting the pool with the surrounding landscape.

Retaining walls: Even in-ground pools may end up aboveground on severe slopes.

SMALL IS BEAUTIFUL

Big Ideas for Small Spaces

Here 'twas as if a weed choked gate
Had greened at my touch, and I had stepped
Into some long forgot, enchanted, strange
Sweet garden of a thousand years ago.
—Edna St. Vincent Millay

Like the small apartment in the big city, the smaller yard or outdoor space offer an exciting challenge to any landscape designer. That said, some of the most beautiful gardens I've seen have been on postage-stamp-size properties, full of the effort and obvious joy of the gardener. From the small properties of Scotland and England to the tiny backyards of many suburbs, I've seen beautiful and lush gardens that celebrate the scale and size rather than diminishing them. These areas might be purposefully created secret gardens formed with hardscape (stone walls, lattice panels, and the like), fences, or green hedges—or sometimes the expanse of the property is simply very small. These spaces create unique challenges as well as wonderful opportunities.

For one thing, this small space may just the spot to do without grass lawn. Chances are that if the space is truly small, it won't support an expanse of open space big enough for recreational activity. In a small-space landscape, lawns sometimes are the paving material of choice, creating soft green paths through the plants and garden features.

Two of the rules of thumb for small spaces: *Keep it simple* and *Find a unifying element or theme.* Generally, repeating a plant or cluster of plants is visually soothing. Too much variation in a small space can be dizzying—there's no visual retreat. I think these same principles apply inside, as does the color scheme. Bold or hot colors can shrink a space, and cool colors should visually expand it. Think of how you approach the decor of the larger and smaller spaces within the house and you'll probably catch on quickly outside.

EXPANDING THE SPACE:

You can create the illusion of depth via the placement of plants and the shape of a garden. Using plant color, texture, and form, you can draw the eye through the garden; with the correct background the viewer is fooled into the seemingly endless depth of foliage. Scale being of primary importance, you might want to choose smaller or dwarf plants. On a smaller scale, once again consider the layering effect on this space and the tendancy to draw the eye though the smaller plants toward larger. Referring to the chapter "Caveat Emptor", choose plants with the word *nana* or *compacta* in the name (dwarf or compact forms). *Gracilus* or *gracillimus* may indicate that a plant is "graceful" in form and would be appropriate for a space like this. There are some beautiful dwarf and pendulous evergreens that can create interest without filling too much space. Deciduous plants often work better in a small space because they are "lighter" and occupy a little less air and light, therefore they're visually less imposing. They allow light to pass through the canopy of their foliage, creating the illusion of depth and distance. Smart plant choice and the simple act of layering can make the boundaries less imposing.

Delicate foliage perennial plants such as ferns, astilbes, columbines, baptisia, or blue fescue can be more appropriate than the large and vigorous leaves of plants like hosta or iris. Look for plants with some detail to their leaf structures (serrated leaves are jagged like the exaggerated edge of a knife) to create interest in detail. The edge of the foliage is what frames the sky or any other view. Large rounded (ovate) leaves can create less interesting negative space. In this case, the negative space just may be the horizon.

Cool colors—white, light pinks, and so forth—can help expand the feeling of the space. These small spaces can be comfortable, well-scaled outdoor rooms if you plan carefully. If you want to establish patios or walkways, use material with smaller inherent scale laid out in simple form. Rather than large flagstone or bluestone, for instance, you may want to use a smaller brick or concrete pavers to create more intricate form and texture. European courtyards are often merely stone paths. The texture of small stone, particularly with the shadows of fine foliage shaking across it, can establish some inherent excitement and beauty.

Keep it Uncomplicated

But like most rules, these can be broken. For a sitting area in a small space you might choose just a few large pieces—bluestone for instance. The simplicity of the layout can make up for the volume of the material. Stick with three or five pieces, or some other odd number depending on the size of the space. It's easy to create dynamic spaces with odd numbers of things, just as easy to slip into static design with even numbers. The small space should be fluid and dynamic, keeping the eye moving easily across it. You

might want to look into the Oriental theory of design called Feng Shui. This is a complete philosophy of simple and calming design for both interior and exterior spaces. In small exterior spaces, the theory is well worth exploring, but in a nutshell it's creating or sustaining a calming and serene environment.

One way to achieve this is to avoid multiple angles, which can create visual tension. Rather, try gentle sweeping curves for your patios, and shapes that are appropriately scaled down. Texture should be fine. Avoid large-leaved rhododendrons or thick and heavy evergreens. Plants like *Acer palmatum* 'Dissectum Viride's (Green Lace leaf Maple) are appropriate because of the delicate foliage and the texture of the deeply cut leaf. Remember, no matter how delicate their scale, some of these plants can get quite big. Read the labels.

Potted plants can help you attain a view on multiple levels, building the gardens up rather than out. These also help you to change the path, both physically and visually by rearrangement.

Informal or rustic shelving can help create this multi-level display and excite the senses. Display hanging vines or even smaller potted plants. Nice rustic shelving has its own visual depth and, weathered down over the years, can form a beautiful screen. Espaliered plants such as climbing hydrangea (*Hydrangea petiolaris*) or firethorn (*Pyracantha*) can dress the walls if the space is limited by some kind of hard structure. Beautiful arbors can create the entry hallway.

Corners can rivet the eye visually. Try planting a cluster of small plants that create depth and draw the eye back toward the forefront or center of the space. Look at paintings to see how successful artists accomplish this. Paul Cézanne said, "Distance is the most important principle of painting." I think what he actually meant is the control of perspective. This is what we need to do in the small space. Inside, this is often accomplished with accent pieces or a cluster of houseplants. (Think *three* rather than *two*.)

The small space can be quite beautiful. For one thing, the garden is all around you. Perspective is singular. There's no stepping back, there's no turning away. The fragrance and color of every leaf and flower change on the slightest breeze, and the movement of the sun is recorded in seconds across the foliage. Quite often grass paths or stepping-stones form the narrow hallways of these spaces. A small clearing or courtyard can give a moment of pause: that very pause we're often searching for in the landscape. That "efficient haven." It is the intimacy of these gardens that is most effective. They are often gardeners' gardens, because there's no looking away from unkind growth, sucker growth, or weeds. So if you surround yourself with a garden in the small space, the relationship is usually a very active one. And this may be why they always seem to be so beautiful and lush.

Scale is of paramount importance in the smaller landscape or garden space. Furniture like benches or chairs should be airy, rather than heavy wood. Or if you use a heavy item then you should choose others sparingly to keep the look uncluttered. Perhaps a wrought-iron bench that allows light to pass through it, casts intricate shadows, and presents small detail to the eye.

Keep the space unified with a binding element of like plants or materials.

Most important, design your space. The smaller the space, the more quickly your impulsiveness will take it over. Use small-leaved plants and soft evergreens to bring things together. Think in soft curves and layers. Careful planning, just as you have to more carefully plan the smaller rooms of your home, is very important with small-space gardening.

Keep it simple.

A BOSTON COURTYARD

Curves and small plants help make this a beautiful space. I designed this to be viewed from a terrace above, the circles and walkways helping to expand the small space. The alpine plants soften the use of stone and brick and help unite the curves.

GOOD FENCES

The art of privacy screening with plants

Before I built a wall I'd ask to know
What I was walling in or walling out,
And to whom I was like to give offense.
—Robert Frost

If you have the space, the key to effective screening with green material is creating a layered planting. Not only will this avoid the intimidating look of a wall, but it should be beautiful, be inviting, and—if done properly—even serve to absorb noise. Quiet neighbors make good neighbors as well. To refer again to Frost, someone who obviously understood both the practicality and beauty of landscape, "Good fences make good neighbors." Rather than accentuate the limits of the property, a "good fence" (in this case, a "green fence") can suggest an endless transition. Before I discuss this in detail, I'll mention some other methods.

There are several ways to screen with plants. The obvious, tried-and-true hedge still works. There are many cases of limited space where this is the only way to solve the privacy dilemma. This usually means a row of evergreen plants that extend above the sight line paraded along the property line.

THE GREEN FENCE

EVERGREENS FOR HEDGING

Ilex (holly): Many of the forms of *Ilex* can provide excellent screens. Look at 'Sky Pencil' or 'steeds' for a fomal border.

Thuja (arborvitae): There are several varieties that can be used effectively. The mature heights and widths vary.

Tsuga canadensis: Canadian hemlock can make a beautiful soft-textured screen where you have some room). It gets quite big—thirty to forty feet tall—and half as wide—so you'll need to leave space or stagger the plants for quicker effect. (*Note:* Hemlocks in some parts of the country are being attacked and damaged by the woolly adelgid.)

DECIDUOUS PLANTS FOR SCREENING

In the northeast, a screening effect may be most important for spring and summer, when the yard is in maximum use. Other times of the year you may want to let as much light in as possible. Here are some plants that "lighten up" in winter, virtually opening up the screen.

Syringa (lilac): Varieties of lilac are fast growing and effective with beautiful fragrant flowers. Varieties grow from five to twenty feet in height.

Vaccinium (highbush blueberries) can make an excellent and useful hedge.

Viburnum varieties, most native to the northeast, can form vigorous masses of nice foliage and flower from three to twenty feet in height.

Multiple-stand screening

Another way to screen is to create primary and secondary stands of plants. Several stands or groupings might create a visual screen without creating an apparently mpenetrable barrier. This can alleviate that feeling that you are sealing the border, making it clear that you're rather trying to salvage some visual privacy or intimacy. As discussed in earlier chapters, you can stake out the location of trees and other plants to visualize their placement. The right placement of just a few trees might create the desired visual barrier.

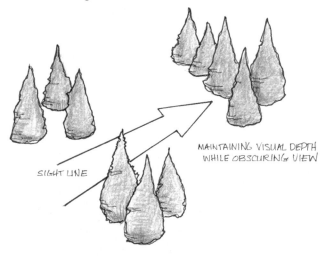

SIGHT LINE

MAINTAINING VISUAL DEPTH WHILE OBSCURING VIEW

The Layered Border

One of the nicest ways to screen, given some space with which to work, is the layered border. Just as the

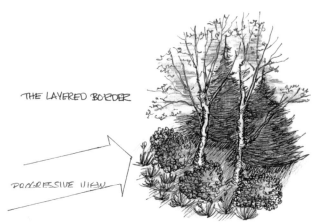

THE LAYERED BORDER

PROGRESSIVE VIEW

forest creates layers, a perimeter screen can be achieved by mixing appropriate plants to create a depth and fullness to the site's edge. If designed and installed correctly, it shouldn't really look like a border at all.

An Intriguing Alternative

E. F. Schumacher, the economist/philosopher/environmentalist, is pioneering something he calls "forest gardening" in England. (Having come full circle, I opened my business with a copy of his *Small Is Beautiful: Economics as if People Mattered* in hand. Now nearly thirty years later I find myself intrigued by the author's philosophy once again.) This involves mimicking the landscape of the forest for residential food production and self-maintenance. Schumacher suggests that following natural succession, all lawns and gardens would return to forest. We are simply preventing this succession by mowing and weeding. Instead we could create a polyculture of plants to produce both beauty and food: nut and fruit trees towering over berry-bearing shrubs and perennial herbs and vegetables, mushrooms covering the understory. These plants can be used for both food and medicine. Birds and butterflies are drawn to the landscape and it becomes self-sustaining. According to the practicing students of this craft, "Forest gardening gives us a visceral experience of ecology in action, teaching us how the planet works and changing our self-perception."

Like I said, intriguing stuff.

A stockade fence softened with a perennial border.

A mixed and layered border for privacy.

KIDSCAPES

user-friendly landscapes
for families with children

Nature wants childredn to be children. . . . Childhood has its own seeing, thinking, feeling.

—Jean-Jacques Rousseau

Landscape beauty and rampant family fun need not be mutually exclusive. Playscapes, sandboxes, and volleyball courts can be beautifully and practically integrated into a wonderful home landscape. The structures themselves can be architecturally attractive, and their placement in the overall scheme can be vital to the enjoyment of the yard—and a big reason we call this slice of land "home." It's great to know the kids can go outdoors within earshot and enjoy some exercise. With our common spaces shrinking in many neighborhoods, the home play area is increasingly important.

Leveling the playing field

One of the first considerations will be whether you have a level space of lawn or other surface that can

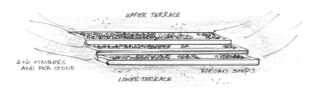

be used for play. If you live on hilly site, you may need to consider some kind of terracing so that a level terrace can be achieved. (See "Ups and Downs.") Safety will be a primary consideration, so think about low terraces with minimum-height retainers. You may want to think about a broad step system. Besides being quite safe, these can present a great place for play and exercise . . . or simply hanging out. And all the while, they're a nice addition to the landscape, which can be upgraded to an adult space in coming years.

Simple berms or raised areas can be fun to climb and safely roll on. These are easy and inexpensive to create. When it comes to play, a varied grade presents opportunity. Kids love to climb. If the slope isn't too severe, consider creating a play area that uses the grade to its advantage. Although they might get expensive, there are custom commercially built systems that can be created to match the site.

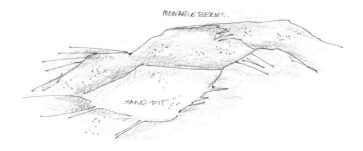

Besides the swimming pool, which we've discussed, there are plenty of other areas to consider for recreation. On a smaller lot, you can find space for a basketball half-court. The traditional driveway system works, but is fraught with the traditional problem of cars parked in the way of the perfect jump shot. With a little innovation you can make the court a part of the private landscape in the backyard. Concrete pavers or some other platform can help you incorporate it into the rear landscape, where you can watch the game without leaning on the car.

Volleyball courts can be constructed with grass or sand. This takes a lot more space, however. You'll need an open, level area of roughly forty feet by seventy feet to accommodate a regulation court.

Kid Landscaping

Any of these features can be landscaped just like other spaces of the yard. For a sandbox / play area for younger children, consider bright-colored flowers and compelling shapes—the same thing you probably did when you designed the bedroom or the playroom. Stimulation, remember? Fragrant flowers and shrubs can help create an inviting area. Flowering

trees like dogwoods can help provide shade to the play area. Trees that might be climbed easily such as beech trees can be established in a recreational area.

Try planting things that attract butterflies such as *Buddleia* (butterfly bush) and *delphinium*. The theory is that masses of a single, bold color attract butterflies and hummingbirds. Sounds like they're a bit like children in that way, doesn't it?

Try working a sandbox (or simply a sand pit) into berms or slopes and all of a sudden you have a great and stimulating play area. Creative retaining systems can add fun to the space.

Consider some garden art or ways to feature the kids' art in the yard. You can build simple partitions and attach painting boards where kids can decorate their own spaces. Perspective and scale remain important elements.

BACK YARD
ART WALLS

BACKYARD SKATING RINK

Ice skating areas can be created by establishing a fairly level area and finding a way to contain a few inches of ice to freeze. Recently I leveled an area about a hundred feet by seventy feet to be longterm useful lawn (for volleyball, soccer, et cetera) and for establishing an ice rink in the winter.

A beautiful stone wall retains the upper terrace. A plastic tarp (available commercially) is framed and filled with 2 to 4 inches of water to freeze over in winter. It will need to be dismantled, so think about storage. I also constructed a "family fire pit" where family and friends can gather for hot chocolate and watch the skating.

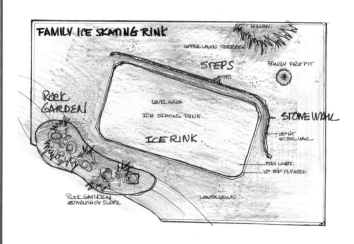

Kids love the intimacy of small spaces, and you can create them without obscuring the view from the house. Look at some whimsical sculptures or safe water features like small fountains that can add to the child's outdoor experience and stimulation. As we discussed earlier, any bold presence diminishes scale. Create a kids' garden. Easy-to-grow species like alpine strawberries and highbush blueberries can teach lessons about the beauty of plants and their ability to provide food. True lavender (*Lavandula angustifolia*) is a beautiful fragrant border for a play area. A shrub border of beach rose (*Rosa Rugosa*) can create a rugged yet beautiful frame for the area.

Elaborate or simple traditional playscapes (swings, slide, and the like) can be custom-designed and -built or purchased. You'll need to prepare some base for the structure; small washed stone or pea stone a few inches deep is the recommended surface. It's actually more forgiving than even bark mulch.

BURNING DESIRES

Gathering around an outdoor fire pit can be a favorite evening tradition. Stone, for its resistance to fire, is the material of choice even for benches. Locate this far from any structures.

A lavender border

Simply put—consider the outdoor environment. Inside the house you've probably gone to great lengths to create a kid-friendly space. Do the same outside the house, and you just may help start children on the path to enjoying the outdoors. You may even inspire a budding landscape designer.

Get the kids involved. Help them imagine and design the space. And by all means, have some fun.

Buddleia "butterfly bush"

196

WHIMSY
Garden accents

A garden without its statue is like a sentence without a verb. —*Joseph W. Beach*

You got to know when to fold. —*Kenny Rogers*

Both sentiments above are perfectly appropriate to for this discussion. I think a focal point of a garden can and possibly should be a work of art. Sculpture has a great history as the anchor of the gardens of antiquity. That said, any accents in the garden are a lot like candy. A little is perfect, while too much is usually way too much. Serious sculpture aside, there is a definite trend toward whimsy in the landscape these days. This lends itself to true enjoyment of the garden, even for those who are not "flower people" in the horticultural sense of the word.

This series of circular elevated patios were constructed on a residential property for the sole purpose of displaying artwork.

I've found gardens and art to combine beautifully. Here a planting of annual impatiens appears to be part of a simple painting I made of of a beach scene .

Black-eyed Susans frame a painting on slate.

I painted and hinged an old window to reflect the natural surroundings. This is used as a privacy screen on a deck.

In a league of his own, sculptor Roger DiTarando creates breathtaking works of art from bronze and copper.

My friend Stan Bonk has been creating pottery meant to be displayed in gardens.

This integration of the arts is nothing new. In fact, is as old as gardening itself. A recent exhibit at Yale University examined the interrelationship between art and music. It opened with "Handel's London: Vauxhall Gardens," which explores the public gardens in London (since the 1600s), "a place of summer strolls accompanied by live music." The *Hartford Courant* went on to say: "Also in the mix at Vauxhall were paintings by artists . . . [the exhibit illustrates] the art of the period is all seen to reference or derive from the gardens." Sculpture in particular has long been a way to add drama to the landscape.

THE SNOW'S LIGHT MADE

Winterscape: the beauty of form, foliage and light

*In the mid-winter evening when the snow's light made
Of the glowing supper hour a blue lost shade.*
—Delmore Schwartz

Where they go is purely beautiful: in the woods in winter, a good coating of snow hides the minor understory vegetation, so the shape of the terrain comes up more clearly. The white background lays an even texture over every declivity, turning the woods into a collection of soft, voluptuous curves—made hard-edged here and there by old stone walls peeping through the snow. . . . The snow's clean plasticity cosmetizes everything, hiding all that messy fertility. I tramp across it enjoying the thought: so many kinds of liveliness under there, also hunkered down, also waiting.

—*John Jerome,* Stone Work

There is no more breathtaking light than that of winter. Turning the snowfields blue and the icy barren branches black, winter creates its own landscape with the brush and knife of freezing wind and fiery sunrise—purple dusk, silvered snow. Whoever said white wasn't a color was right. It is a thousand colors shivering, waiting to be unveiled.

Winter simplifies—visually, at least. Take a room full of furniture and artifacts and throw a soft, perfectly white sheet over the whole thing. That's winter. With the room covered in sheets what's left is not the detail of the shapes but small and large forms, the shadows they cast, the light they absorb or reflect. One of the beauties of winter is the transformation. The sheet isn't cast all at once but rather gathers, rummaging through the empty spaces between things, filling darkness with light. Watch a blue spruce being draped in snow: the negative space becomes the image of the tree, layered white between the soft edges of the spruce branches. It fills until it is overcome with the blanket of snow and then might vanish into a heavy storm. But by the next afternoon, the layered silver bending under the weight emerges slowly to the afternoon sun, and the shape and texture are transformed once again.

Watch the low foliage of the perennials or the low shrubs emerge from the white. The green is greener, the brown terrestrial. The melting snow forms swelling circles around the trees, and the shrubs and the circles intertwine, forming a pale, intricate mosaic across the ground. Watch this lesson in scale as bare ground emerges and the shadows shrink. Watch the simplicity of the lines and curves left by the melting snow. I am sure there is a lesson here. I'm sure the curves of our landscape should be no more severe than the gentle sweeps of receding snow. "All art is but an imitation of nature."

For the residential landscape, consider form in the yard. When the blanket's drawn over, what's left to see? If a flat plane of white is what you desire, then this is easy to achieve. If you would like to add some drama to the winter landscape, choose shrubs and trees with interesting architectural form. In the simplified canvas of winter, these forms can be startling.

Rock gardens add a great deal of interest: Snow melts earlier on rock than it does on soil, creating a pattern of its own. Retaining heat, the stone might emerge alone, before all of the surrounding elements.

Consider this in the "in the stripped end of winter," when the landscape has been simplified by dormancy and snow.

Canadian hemlock (*Tsuga*)

Winterberry (*ilex verticillata*)

The fine detail of barberry in winter

The early winter color of leucothoe.

In the winterscape, *line* emerges as color recedes.

In the depth of winter lies the promise of the seasons to come.

Photo by Randy Anagnostis

A CAPACITY FOR WONDER
Conclusion

For a transitory moment man must have held his breath in the presence of this continent, compelled into an aesthetic contemplation he neither understood nor desired, face to face for the last time in history with something commensurate to his capacity for wonder.
—*F. Scott Fitzgerald,* The Great Gatsby

I have always wondered at the true value of what we do as designers and landscapers; how we dare mimic or even alter the natural world. Ours is at best, as is perhaps all art, an attempt to mimic the natural world. I trust if you've gotten this far that you've enjoyed—or at least tolerated—the premise of this book. Although I've made a decent living at the craft of landscaping, it is the art that continues to intrigue me, and I hope that has come across in my explanations and explorations of what exactly are landscape design and landscape gardening/construction. This

is an inexact science if it is a science at all. It is fraught with errors, and in the case of the residential landscape your yard is your laboratory. You will be learning in perpetuity from both your successes and your failures.

Hopefully the brief discussions and illustrations included in this book will help you avoid some of the errors and enjoy more of the rewards. I truly believe, more now than ever, that this kind of work should be done with great joy and have as its result something akin to a catharsis. I have tried to relate garden design to the other arts: poetry, literature, painting, sculpture, and even music. I can imagine the raised eyebrows and the shaking heads, but I believe in the connection of all these creative exercises. We approach something sacred when we dare create.

Design, gardening, masonry, and carpentry are all wonderfully creative endeavors. And with knowledge at our fingertips and imagination in our minds, landscaping practiced as an art is an illumination of the soul. Even if we are unaware of it, the creation of the gardens and paths around us can become the framework of our lives. It can be subtle or bold, calming or exhilarating, reflecting something of who, at some perhaps unexamined level, we truly are.

In the end the successful landscape is one considered with an artist's eye. Remember, my premise is that landscaping is as much an *art*, arguably moreso, as it is a *craft*. And as with most art, there should be included an element of joy. There are wonderful professionals in the industry: horticulturists, masons, landscape contractors and passionate gardeners who embrace gardening as a way of life. And though the elusive green thumb may be the part of the human anatomy mentioned most in relation to gardening, there is no question that when it comes to landscape and garden design, the inspired soul is called on. It is creative expression, no less than painting or poetry or sculpture. In fact, Goethe, the eighteenth- and nineteenth-century novelist, artist, philosopher, politician—who clearly saw few separations among the creative arts—once referred to architecture as "frozen music."

Use all your senses when landscaping. It is a wonderful, creative process. It's your particular and informed view. In this case—"the eyes have it."

Landscape design is an art. Amen.

I swear the earth shall be complete to him or her who
shall be complete;
The earth remains jagged and broken only to him or her who
remains jagged or broken.

—*Walt Whitman,* Leaves of Grass